Introduction to
LITERARY
TERMS
With Exercises

SHARON HAMILTON

Peoples
education
Your partner in student success™

About the Author

Sharon Hamilton (Ph.D. University of Illinois at Urbana-Champaign) has taught college literature courses at Eastern Michigan, Baylor, and Hunter, and Advanced Placement English at Phillips Exeter Academy and the Buckingham Browne & Nichols School, where she currently teaches. She is an award-winning teacher, NEH teaching workshop leader, and an Advanced Placement English Consultant for the College Board. She recently wrote *Essential Literary Terms With Exercises*, published by Peoples Education and W. W. Norton and Company. She is also the author of *Shakespeare's Daughters* and *Shakespeare: A Teaching Guide*, as well as multiple books on solving common writing problems.

Executive Editor: Doug Falk

Editor: Carol Alexander

Director of Editorial Services: Lee Laddy

Copy Editor: Shelly Rawson

Production Director: Jason Grasso

Assistant Production Manager: Steven Genzano

Book Design: Anna Palchik

Permissions Manager: Kristine Liebman

Marketing Manager: Marcie Silver

Your partner in student success™   **ISBN   978-1-4138-9480-6**

Manufactured in Newburyport, MA in July 2012 by Bradford & Bigelow, Inc.

Printed in the United States of America.

10   9   8   7   6

Contents

III

▼

▼

To the Student

Introduction to Literary Terms With Exercises was inspired by the assumption that English classes need a source for clear definitions of frequently used terms and concepts—those that come up frequently in discussion—so that readers have a common vocabulary for discussing poetry and fiction. It also helps readers to see patterns, to get past a superficial initial response of "I like it" or "It's funny" and begin to see the art behind the work.

A guide to literary terms can encourage readers to categorize and to compare, the essence of critical thinking. Once introduced to the concept of metaphor, for example, readers have a basis for understanding how one poet's use of it differs from another's. Once they learn to identify a sonnet, they are prepared to see how that poetic form can serve multiple subjects and express totally different tones. Finally, a good guidebook can also provide a sense of heritage, by presenting techniques and approaches that authors have used in the past.

This book defines and explains the most essential terms in a clear, straightforward style. It also provides numerous examples and exercises to test and develop understanding. The exercises in each chapter give readers practice in identifying the techniques that are key to understanding the tone and meaning of a literary passage. In addition, the analyses of passages that accompany the explanations of the terms serve as models. They offer examples of how the terms may be used in writing precise and detailed literary analysis. With its emphasis on application—how writers use literary techniques and how readers can identify and analyze them—this book guides users to a surer understanding of literature.

How to Use This Book

This book is designed for quick and easy reference. Terms are grouped by topic. It begins with those that apply broadly to imaginative writing in all genres (Literary Forms, Figurative Language, Rhetorical Strategies). Then it moves to topics that are more specific to prose (Narration, Structure, Syntax). Finally, it deals with topics that are more specific to poetry (Rhythm and Meter, Rhyme, Sound and Sound Patterns, and Poetic Forms). Within these groupings, terms are arranged to show patterns and connections. A reader may look up either an individual term, like **simile**, or an entire group of terms—for example, all the entries under the category **figurative language**. If one term is more important or accessible than the others, it is listed first. For example, the most easily understood category of **figures of**

▼

thought, **simile**, is given first, followed by the related, more complex
class, **metaphor**. Those major **tropes** are followed by such subsets
as **personification** and **pathetic fallacy**. If two terms are related—for
example, **first-person** and **third-person**, both of which describe a
point of view—the table of contents lists them in consecutive order. If
no order of importance applies, as in the terms associated with **structure**, the listing within the category is alphabetical. The one exception
to this arrangement is the section on **rhythm and meter**. It is clearest
if read as a whole, although each term can still be studied on its own.
The discussions of individual terms also cross-reference related terms,
which are indicated by small capital letters. An index in the back of
the book allows readers to quickly locate a particular literary term.

Exercises that both test and enhance the reader's understanding and
ability to apply the terms in context reinforce study of the definitions
and examples. The exercises focus on brief passages that ask readers to
perform three tasks:
  • to identify the literary term or terms that the passage illustrates
  • to explain why that term applies
  • to discuss how the technique affects the meaning and tone of
    the passage

Why You Should Use This Book

The goals of this book are brevity, clarity, and selectivity. Students
should be able to turn to it for a clear understanding of key terms
needed to read and analyze the classics and their modern heirs. At the
same time, *Introduction to Literary Terms With Exercises* offers more
than dictionary-style definitions by providing exercises to identify and
discuss. The book will demonstrate how a poetic line is an example
of, say, alliteration and why the use of that device matters to the line's
meaning. In other words, the purpose is to go beyond simply assign-
ing a label—the what—to speculate on the how and the why.

On the most basic level, readers need to learn the major ways that
the style of fiction and poetry differ from that of ordinary prose. This distinction is not an absolute, as shades of differences, some obvious, some
subtle, exist between everyday and literary style. The most workaday
sorts of writing are intended simply to explain or inform: they may, for
example, provide directions on how to operate an automobile. Such writ-
ings avoid any hint of an author's distinctive voice and any deviation from
the literal. Those qualities would only detract from the major aim, clarity.
When an additional goal becomes to persuade, however, ordinary usage
borrows some of the devices of literary style. That happens, for example,
in ads, political speeches, and editorials. Such writing strives not simply
to inform but also to influence its audience. For example, directions in
a national park about how to avoid attracting bears may contain vivid

imagery, and some passages in great novels, plays, and poems are models of clear statement.

Another way of putting this point is that how something is said is crucial to what it means. The old saying defines poetry as the genre in which style is inseparable from content, a concept that could also be applied to fiction and drama. Good readers sense such factors, but they must be encouraged to identify and explain their perceptions. They must go back to a piece that they have responded to instinctively and look for ways that the style has influenced the effect. It is in the nuances, the subtext created by word choice, structure, rhythm, and sound, that full meaning resides. Of course a work may evoke more than one meaning, as well as several levels of related meanings. In fact, one test of a book's richness is the increasingly complex understanding that can be gained from repeated readings and from discussion with other readers.

Introduction to Literary Terms With Exercises benefits from a long and rich heritage. Authors have used the literary concepts and techniques that the book describes for thousands of years, before literature had even assumed a written form. For nearly as long, scholars, feeling the need to order and describe their responses to that art, have labeled, classified, and analyzed these concepts and techniques. This book will offer students the chance not simply to memorize literary terms but to apply them in context, and to explore ways in which knowledge of how they work can enrich meaning. It is a means to ends that go beyond the classroom: to enhance literary sensibility and to foster skills that can lead to a lifetime of informed and pleasurable reading.

To the Teacher

Introduction to Literary Terms With Exercises is an abridged and simplified version of *Essential Literary Terms*, published jointly by Peoples Education and W. W. Norton in 2007. The impetus for this new book was the request of many teachers for a guide aimed at ninth- and tenth-grade students, as opposed to those in the upper grades of high school and in college who were the intended audience for its predecessor. The two books share the same assumptions and techniques, described in the section "To the Student," which is directed at both teachers and students. Again, the explanations and illustrations of terms are followed by exercises that ask students to apply that information to a select number of passages from literary works, classic and modern. As in the earlier book, a set of *Answers to Exercises* is available to teachers as support.

This book includes few exercises on the analysis of long, complex passages that appear in *Essential Literary Terms*. Instead, it aims to build the foundation that will allow for that more advanced critical analysis later on. In that sense, it is meant to complement the goals and content of pre-AP English classes.

In other important ways, too, *Introduction to Literary Terms With Exercises* reflects those aims and that audience. The syntax has been simplified and the vocabulary modified for greater reading ease. Some relatively rare or specialized literary terms, such as "chiasmus" and "catalexis," have been cut. In other cases, the most complex application of a term or extensive information on its history have been eliminated—for example, the broader, kinesthetic sense of "onomatopoeia" and the account of the development of the novel.

In several of the examples, both in the text and in the exercises, more age-appropriate passages have been substituted. For example, Shakespearean plays more frequently read in ninth and tenth grades, such as *Romeo and Juliet* and *Macbeth*, have been used in place of works more often taught in the upper grades, such as *Othello* and *Antony and Cleopatra*. The number, complexity, and length of the sample passages have been revised to suit the experience and reading level of younger students. Some parts of the earlier text, such as the section of the preface describing the structure and scoring of the English Literature AP Examination and the appendix on the MLA style of documentation, have been cut altogether. The assumption is that those topics should be directed at older, more advanced students.

The result of these editing choices is a briefer, more portable book. It aims to address a younger audience in a way that they can readily comprehend. At the same time, great care has been taken to maintain the clarity and rigor of its predecessor.

Author Acknowledgments

I want to thank Jim Peoples for the proposal that I write this book and the staff at Peoples Education for their support. Particular gratitude goes to Carol Alexander, my editor, for her thoughtful and efficient guidance. I also want to recognize the many teachers, colleagues, and students who have inspired my work.

Literary Forms

Literature may be divided into three major **literary forms**: POETRY, FICTION, and DRAMA. POETRY is usually categorized into three main types: EPIC, DRAMATIC, and LYRIC. All three subtypes share common traits, including specific patterns of RHYTHM and SYNTAX, frequent use of FIGURATIVE language, and emphasis on the way that words are arranged on the page. Although some works of FICTION and DRAMA also display these traits, they are particularly characteristic of POETRY.

FICTION is, in general, any NARRATIVE about invented characters and events, whether in VERSE or prose. The narrower meaning of the term, however, refers to works written in prose. The major genres of fiction are the **novel**, the **short story**, and the **novella**.

DRAMA differs from POETRY and FICTION in that it is usually intended for performance. The form may be divided into the broad categories of COMEDY and TRAGEDY. A third and smaller category, TRAGICOMEDY, combines features of each of those major genres.

DRAMA

Drama is the major LITERARY FORM that presents characters directly to the audience, usually without the presence of a NARRATOR. Most drama is written to be performed in the theater by live actors, who speak the DIALOGUE and move in accordance with the STAGE DIRECTIONS written by the **playwright**—literally, the maker of the **play**.

Drama is classified according to the overall effect intended on the audience, as well as the choice and use of the material to achieve that effect: The broadest division is that between COMEDY and TRAGEDY.

Some plays, comic and tragic, are written in VERSE. ELIZABETHAN dramas, composed during the reign of England's Queen Elizabeth I (1558–1603), often used this form. Many of these plays were written almost entirely in BLANK VERSE, that is, UNRHYMED IAMBIC PENTAMETER. William Shakespeare was the master of verse drama in the Elizabethan age. Some modern examples of verse plays are T.S. Eliot's *Murder in the Cathedral* (1935) and Archibald MacLeish's *J.B.: A Play in Verse.*

Most students encounter plays in their written form. This form can be an advantage. Readers have the opportunity to review the cast of characters, key sections of DIALOGUE, and STAGE DIRECTIONS that indicate the actions and the vocal inflections of the characters.

On the other hand, it can be difficult for a reader to distinguish among the voices of the characters or to picture the physical movements that accompany the words. A reader may tend to read a play as one long **monologue**, a long speech by a single character. Seeing a performance of the play can help a reader understand the written form. It is important to remember, however, that every performance represents a series of choices, by the director and the actors, about such factors as which lines to cut or to emphasize; how the roles are cast; how the actors should move, gesture, and deliver their lines; and how the SETTING, the time and place in which the action occurs, is represented.

Nowhere is the range of possibilities open to directors and actors so clear as in productions of Shakespeare's plays. Because most have continued to be staged during the four hundred years since they were written and because they contain few stage directions, productions of Shakespeare have inspired a wide variety of choices about styles and settings. For example, the TRAGEDY *Romeo and Juliet* has been set everywhere from Elizabethan England to Renaissance Italy to modern-day Verona to Verona Beach, California. The last setting, in the film version directed by Baz Luhrmann (1997), was complete with rival teenage gangs driving hotrods, wearing punk outfits, and armed with switchblades and guns. Even if a production is strikingly effective or innovative for its day, however, its effect is inevitably short-lived. The written text, in contrast, remains to inspire future visions of the play, on stage and in readers' imaginations.

See also NARRATION, CHARACTERIZATION, DIALOGUE, SOLILOQUY, and ASIDE.

► Comedy

In **comedy**, the TONE is for the most part light, and the main effect is to entertain the audience. The situations and characters tend to be drawn from ordinary daily life, as opposed to world-shaking events and noble or royal characters. Also, the resolution is happy, at least for the major characters. Many comedies conclude with the marriage of one or more couples. Although the term "comedy" applies primarily to drama, it is also used to describe the type of plot in PROSE FICTION and NARRATIVE POETRY.

▼

Comedy may be divided into a wide range of types. One major category is "low" comedy, which depends on physical humor, fast-paced action, ridiculous caricatures, and crude jests. It includes such plays as Shakespeare's *The Comedy of Errors* and the Three Stooges films. "High" comedy, in contrast, depends largely on witty dialogue among sophisticated characters. Examples include Shakespeare's *As You Like It* and *Twelfth Night* and Oscar Wilde's *The Importance of Being Earnest*. Many high comedies, however, contain low comic features as well.

Tragedy ◄

In **tragedy**, the *tone* is serious and often somber. The effect is to involve and strongly move the audience. The outcome is disastrous for the PROTAGONIST and, often, also for those associated with him or her. The resolution of a tragedy often involves one or more deaths, in particular that of the PROTAGONIST. His or her fate is more moving if the faults of character that bring it about are minor in comparison with the suffering created. Tragedies range from classical examples from ancient Greece, such as *Oedipus Rex* and *Antigone,* to such Elizabethan plays as Shakespeare's *Romeo and Juliet* and *Macbeth*. Modern examples include Henrik Ibsen's *Hedda Gabler* (1890) and Arthur Miller's *Death of a Salesman* (1949).

Tragicomedy ◄

Some plays, called **tragicomedies**, fall in the middle of the tragic/comic spectrum. They focus on both high and low characters and situations, and they bring a potentially tragic plot to a happy resolution, at least for the PROTAGONIST. The means is a sudden reversal of fortune or the reformation of the protagonist's opponent. This form was especially popular in ELIZABETHAN drama. Examples include Shakespeare's *Measure for Measure* (1604) and *All's Well that Ends Well* (1602–03), sometimes called "dark comedies" or "problem comedies."

FICTION

In a broad sense, **fiction** is any narrative, whether written in verse or in prose, about invented characters and events, as opposed to an account of actual happenings. The latter category, which includes such subheadings as history and biography, is called **nonfiction**. The narrower and more common definition of fiction, however, refers to stories written in prose.

Fiction includes three major types: the NOVEL, a narrative of varying lengths but usually long enough for separate publication; the SHORT STORY, nearly always published in a collection of such pieces or in a magazine; and the NOVELLA, a narrative whose length falls between those of the other two types and which may or may not be published in an individual volume. All three types share certain traits. They focus on a character or characters that interact in a given social SETTING, and they are narrated from a particular POINT OF VIEW. They are also based on some sort of PLOT, a series of events leading to a resolution that is designed to reveal aspects of the characters. The main tone may be comic, tragic, satiric, or romantic.

Novel

The **novel**, because of its greater length and scope, is much more complex than the SHORT STORY. Its plot is typically more involved, its description of the society more complete, and its depiction of characters' motives, feelings, and experiences more complex than the concise SHORT STORY form allows. A major early inspiration for the novel was the Spanish writer Miguel de Cervantes's *Don Quixote* (1605). In English literature, the form was introduced in such books as Daniel Defoe's adventure novel *Robinson Crusoe* (1719) and Samuel Richardson's *Pamela* (1740), written as a series of letters. Later examples include an enormous range of subjects and styles, from Jane Austen's *Pride and Prejudice* to Fyodor Dostoevsky's *Crime and Punishment* to Ernest Hemingway's *A Farewell to Arms* to Jhumpa Lahiri's *The Namesake*.

▼

Short Story

◀

The **short story** shares with the novel several characteristics of fiction, but its more concentrated form results in some important differences. These include a smaller cast of characters, often focusing on the PRO-TAGONIST; a simpler plot, usually centered on a single major conflict; a limited depiction of SETTING; and a briefer format, with descriptive details and DIALOGUE selected for maximum significance and effect. Edgar Allan Poe, one of the early masters of the short story form, defined it as a work that could be read in one session of no more than two hours and that was focused on creating "a single effect."

Novella

◀

The **novella** falls between the novel and the short story in both length and complexity. A particular novella may be substantial enough to be published in a separate volume, like a NOVEL, or, in other circumstances, concise enough to be included in a collection of other relatively short pieces. Some masterpieces of the form include Herman Melville's *Billy Budd* (1890), Kate Chopin's *The Awakening* (1899), Joseph Conrad's *Heart of Darkness* (1902), James Joyce's *The Dead* (1914), Franz Kafka's *The Metamorphosis* (1915), and Nella Larsen's *Passing* (1929).

POETRY

Poetry has been defined in different ways—for example, as the form in which style is inseparable from content. In *The Norton Anthology of Poetry,* the poet and critic Jon Stallworthy offers a helpful defini-tion: "A poem is a composition written for performance by the human voice." He notes that responding to a poem fully requires not only understanding the meaning of the words but also sensing the ways that their sounds, rhythms, and arrangement interact. One means of access is to hear the poem, either by reading it aloud or by listening to it read by the poet or by a performer. At least, one should try to hear it in one's mind or imagination—let the poem, in Keats's PARADOXICAL description in "Ode to a Nightingale," "pipe to the spirit ditties of no sound." Although attentive listening may not yield the entire meaning,

▼

especially of a complex poem, it can emphasize aspects of the sound that give important insights into the sense of the words.

Poetry is usually divided into three main types: EPIC, DRAMATIC, and LYRIC. All three types of poetry share certain common traits: an emphasis on the connections between the sound and sense of words; controlled patterns of rhythm and syntax; vivid, often figurative language; and close attention to the effects of the arrangement of words on the page. Although many of these characteristics also apply to FICTION and DRAMA, and even to ordinary prose, they are particularly concentrated in poetry. That literary form is often used to express heightened feeling or subtle thought, even though sometimes the tone may be comic or the subject matter mundane. Some critics use the term "verse" to distinguish light or trivial pieces from the more serious and highly developed works of "poetry."

Epic Poetry

An epic is a long narrative poem on a serious and exalted subject, such as man's fall from heavenly grace in John Milton's *Paradise Lost*. Ancient and medieval epics, such as Homer's *Iliad* and the anonymous *Beowulf* in the West and *Gilgamesh* and *The Mahabharata* in the East, recount the deeds of a cultural hero. They combine legend, oral history, and moral lesson to inspire and guide future generations. Such epics began as oral performances, chanted or sung to the accompaniment of an instrument like the lyre. During generations of performance, they were shaped and refined by multiple bards and were finally recorded in written form. The more recent epics that these early works inspired, such as Milton's *Paradise Lost*, were composed in written form by a single author.

Dramatic Poetry

Dramatic poetry is that in which the writer creates the voice of an invented character or characters. In its simplest form, it is a monologue, such as Robert Browning's "My Last Duchess," in which the narrator is an egocentric and unscrupulous Italian duke, or Langston Hughes's "Mother to Son," in which the speaker is a resilient black woman giving advice to a young son. The most complex form of dramatic poetry is the full-length verse play, in which multiple speakers are given distinctive voices. The master of the form was William Shakespeare.

▼

Lyric Poetry ◄

Lyric poetry, the most varied and widespread kind, is that in which an individual speaker expresses what he or she feels, perceives, and thinks. It includes poems as diverse as Shakespeare's sonnets, Keats's odes, and Sylvia Plath's "Daddy." Although the usual point of view is first person, it is important to distinguish the "I" of the speaker from that of the actual poet; however close the speaker may seem to be to the poet's point of view, he or she is always in some part an invented character. **Lyrics** are usually short, especially in comparison to the other forms of poetry, but some, such as Walt Whitman's "Song of Myself," may extend to several pages.

SPECIALIZED FORMS

The major literary forms of poetry and fiction contain specialized forms with distinctive elements and styles. The dramatic monologue is a specialized form of poetry, for example, and satire is a specialized form of both poetry and fiction.

Dramatic Monologue ◄

A **dramatic monologue** is a poem that is spoken by a FICTIONAL NARRATOR who is clearly different from the author in age, situation, or gender. It is set at some significant point in the speaker's life, and it is often addressed to another character, whose presence is implied by what the speaker says. The major purpose of a dramatic monologue is for the speaker to reveal, often unknowingly, significant aspects of his or her qualities, values, and experiences, which are inferred by the reader. The form came to prominence in the work of the Victorian poet Robert Browning, whose "My Last Duchess," "Fra Lippo Lippi," and "Porphyria's Lover" are classic examples.

In "My Last Duchess," for example, the speaker is an arrogant Italian Renaissance duke showing a visitor around his palazzo. The palace contains an extensive collection of artworks, of which a portrait of his late wife seems merely an example, until he hints at its darker significance. As the duke speaks, he reveals that he is

▼

irritated by the animated look that the painter has captured, seeing it as evidence of "a heart . . . too soon made glad, / Too easily impressed." The duke did not call the duchess's attention to what he saw as a fault—her universal good will, rather than an exclusive preference for his "gift of a nine-hundred-years-old name." That would have been to "stoop" to her simple level, and, the duke proclaims arrogantly, "I choose / Never to stoop." The consequence was that he "gave commands" and then "all smiles stopped together." His meaning is slyly ambiguous: Did his oppressive treatment drive his young wife to fatal despair? Or were the "commands" of a more violent nature: an order to stop her smiles by ending her life?

Other examples of dramatic monologues are T. S. Eliot's "The Love Song of J. Alfred Prufrock," in which the NARRATOR is a prudish, self-conscious guest at a cocktail party, and several poems in which the speakers are literary characters, whom the poet imagines outside the work in which they originally appear. For example, many dramatic monologues have been inspired by Homer's *The Odyssey*, including Tennyson's *Ulysses*, spoken by the hero in old age, and Margaret Atwood's "Siren Song," narrated by a modern version of one of the harpies, who tries to lure Odysseus to his death with her song. See also UNRELIABLE NARRATOR.

EXERCISE: Dramatic Monologue

For the following DRAMATIC MONOLOGUE:
- Describe the point in the speaker's life at which it is set.
- Describe the nature of the implied audience.
- Discuss the revelations that the speech provides about the NARRATOR'S personality traits, values, and experiences.

> Well, son, I'll tell you:
> Life for me ain't been no crystal stair.
> It's had tacks in it,
> And splinters,
> And boards torn up,   5
> And places with no carpet on the floor—
> Bare.
> But all the time
> I'se been a-climbin' on,
> And reachin' landin's,   10
> And turnin' corners,
> And sometimes goin' in the dark

Where there ain't been no light.
So boy, don't you turn back.
Don't you set down on the steps   15
'Cause you finds it's kinder hard.
Don't you fall now—
For I'se still goin', honey,
I'se still climbin',
And life for me ain't been no crystal stair.   20
               —LANGSTON HUGHES, "Mother to Son"

Satire   ◄

Satire is a genre of COMEDY that is directed at ridiculing human faults
and vices, such as vanity, hypocrisy, stupidity, and greed. It differs
from pure comedy in that the aim is not simply to evoke laughter, but
to expose and criticize such faults, often with the aim of correcting
them. The target of the satire may vary. In some works, it is a particular individual, as in John Dryden's "Mac Flecknoe" (1682, 1684),
directed at a fellow playwright, Thomas Shadwell, whom Dryden
depicts as dull and self-satisfied. Other satires target a group or set of
people, such as the members of the American military establishment
in Joseph Heller's *Catch-22* (1961), or an institution, such as totalitarianism in George Orwell's *Animal Farm* (1946). Some satires even aim
at the whole of humanity—for example, Book IV of Jonathan Swift's
Gulliver's Travels (1726). That section of the novel is set on an imaginary island, which is inhabited by two radically opposed species. The
brutish Yahoos have the outward form of human beings, while their
masters, the Houyhnhnms, are talking horses who have the human
intelligence that the Yahoos entirely lack.

A useful means of categorizing satire is into "direct" and "indirect" forms. In **direct satire**, also called **formal satire**, the FIRST-PER-
SON NARRATOR addresses a specific audience, either the reader or an
invented listener, whom he or she expects will sympathize with the
views expressed. For example, in Lord Byron's mock epic, *Don Juan*
(1824), the sophisticated narrator confides to the reader the romantic adventures of Don Juan, a legendary seducer, in his youth; Byron
depicts him as naïve and irresistibly attractive.

Indirect satire, the usual mode of ridicule in satiric PLAYS and
works of PROSE FICTION, is not presented in the form of a direct
address to the audience. Rather, the criticism of the characters'
vices and follies is implied by simply representing their thoughts,
words, and actions. The oldest known indirect satires are those of

▼

the ancient Greek playwright Aristophanes (c.450–c.385 B.C.E.), who wrote such satiric depictions of Athenian society as *The Frogs* and *The Clouds*. Other examples include Ben Jonson's satire on vanity and greed, *Volpone* (1606); Richard Brinsley Sheridan's witty exposure of adultery and hypocrisy in London high society, *The School for Scandal* (1777); and Evelyn Waugh's *The Loved One* (1948), a clever depiction of shallowness, greed, and excessive sentimentality, set at a pet cemetery in Hollywood.

Although satire began with the plays of Aristophanes, the main founders of the form were two Roman poets, Horace (65–68 B.C.E.) and Juvenal (c.65–c.135 C.E.). Each wrote a distinctive type of satire that has given its name to and inspired the two major categories of later satiric works.

Horatian satire is tolerant and sophisticated, indulgently mocking faults with the aim of evoking wry amusement rather than repulsion or indignation in the audience. Some examples include Alexander Pope's "The Rape of the Lock" (1712), which gently ridicules the vanity and idleness of the British upper classes in the form of a mock epic on the supposed tragedy of the lovely Belinda, a lock of whose hair is ravished by the scissors of a wicked Baron; Lord Byron's *Don Juan* (1819), mentioned above; and the Emmeline Grangerford episode in Mark Twain's *Adventures of Huckleberry Finn* (1884), in which Twain pokes fun at the preoccupation with death in the sentimental drawings and verse of an adolescent would-be poet.

Juvenalian satire, in contrast, is harsh and judgmental, bitterly condemning vices and faults and inciting the audience to feelings of indignation and even disgust. Examples of Juvenalian satire include Samuel Johnson's "The Vanity of Human Wishes" (1749) and Mark Twain's *Pudd'nhead Wilson* (1894), a sharp condemnation of the injustices of slavery. A supreme example of the form is Jonathan Swift's "A Modest Proposal" (1729). In it the author denounces the exploitation of peasants in his native Ireland by absentee British landlords, who were indifferent to the suffering they were causing and who were supported by the apathy of the British parliament and monarchy. Swift's NARRATOR is a coldly logical social commentator, who advocates combating overpopulation and hunger by what he sees as the inspired plan of using the babies of the poor as food.

EXERCISE: Satire

For each of the following examples:

- State whether the satire is FORMAL (DIRECT) or INDIRECT. If it is direct, describe the nature of the audience to whom it is addressed.
- Identify the type of SATIRE that it exemplifies, HORATIAN or JUVENALIAN, and justify that choice of category.
- Explain the targets of the SATIRE: the human vice[s] or fault[s] and the person, institution, or group at which it is aimed.

1.   All human things are subject to decay,
And when fate summons, monarchs must obey.
This Flecknoe[1] found, who, like Augustus, young
Was called to empire, and had governed long;
In prose and verse, was owned, without dispute,   5
Through all the realms of Nonsense, absolute.
This agèd prince, now flourishing in peace,
And blest with issue of a large increase,[2]
Worn out with business, did at length debate
To settle the succession of the state;   10
And, pondering which of all his sons was fit
To reign, and wage immortal war with wit,
Cried: "'Tis resolved; for Nature pleads that he
Should only rule, who most resembles me.
Sh——[3] alone, of all my sons, is he   15
Who stands confirmed in full stupidity.
The rest to some faint meaning make pretense,
But Sh—— never deviates into sense."

                                   —JOHN DRYDEN, "Mac Flecknoe"

2. By the time you swear you're his,
      Shivering and sighing,
And he vows his passion is
      Infinite, undying—
Lady, make a note of this: 5
      One of you is lying.

                    —DOROTHY PARKER, "Unfortunate Coincidence"

---

1. Richard Flecknoe, an Irish poet Dryden considered dull.
2. Children; also, Flecknoe's practice of republishing old works under new titles.
3. Thomas Shadwell, a playwright and rival of Dryden.

▼

3.   *In this section of* Adventures of Huckleberry Finn, *Huck, the* NARRATOR, *has just seen Buck Grangerford, his new friend and the son of his generous host, shoot at "a splendid young man" from the other prominent local family, the Shepherdsons. Buck's father, Col. Grangerford, clearly approves of the attack. Huck takes the first opportunity to question the other boy about the situation.*

"Did you want to kill him, Buck?"

"Well, I bet I did."

"What did he do to you?"

"Him? He never done nothing to me."

"Well, then, what did you want to kill him for?"

"Why nothing—only it's on account of the feud."

"What's a feud?"

"Why, where was you raised? Don't you know what a feud is?"

"Never heard of it before—tell me about it."

"Well," says Buck, "a feud is this way. A man has a quarrel with another man, and kills him; then that other man's brother kills *him*; then the other brothers, on both sides, goes for one another; then the *cousins* chip in—and by and by everybody's killed off, and there ain't no more feud. But it's kind of slow, and takes a long time."

"Has this one been going on long, Buck?"

"Well I should *reckon*! it started thirty year ago, or som'ers along there. There was trouble 'bout something and then a lawsuit to settle it; and the suit went agin one of the men, and so he up and shot the man that won the suit—which he would naturally do, of course. Anybody would."

"What was the trouble about, Buck?—land?"

"I reckon maybe—I don't know."

"Well, who done the shooting?—was it a Grangerford or a Shepherdson?"

"Laws, how do *I* know? it was so long ago."

–MARK TWAIN, *Adventures of Huckleberry Finn*

4.   MRS. CANDOUR Mr. Surface, what news do you hear?—though indeed it is no matter, for I think one hears nothing else but scandal.

JOSEPH SURFACE Just so, indeed, madam.

MRS. CANDOUR Ah, Maria! child,—what, is the whole affair off between you and Charles? His extravagance, I presume—the town talks of nothing else.

MARIA I am very sorry, ma'am, the town has so little to do.

MRS. CANDOUR True, true, child: but there is no stopping people's tongues. I own I was hurt to hear it, as indeed I was to learn, from the same quarter, that your guardian, Sir Peter, and Lady Teazle have not agreed lately so well as could be wished. . . .

MARIA Such reports are highly scandalous.

MRS. CANDOUR So they are, child—shameful, shameful! But the world is so censorious, no character escapes. Lord, now who would have suspected your friend, Miss Prim, of an indiscretion? Yet such is the ill-nature of people, that they say her uncle stopped her last week, just as she was stepping into the York Diligence[4] with her dancing-master.

MARIA I'll answer for't there are no grounds for the report.

MRS. CANDOUR Oh, no foundation in the world, I dare swear; no more, than for the story circulated last month, of Mrs. Festino's affair with Colonel Cassino;—though, to be sure, that matter was never rightly cleared up.

JOSEPH SURFACE The license of invention some people take is monstrous indeed.

MARIA 'Tis so.—But, in my opinion, those who report such things are equally culpable.

MRS. CANDOUR To be sure they are; tale-bearers are as bad as the tale-makers—'tis an old observation, and a very true one—but what's to be done, as I said before? how will you prevent people from talking?
—RICHARD BRINSLEY SHERIDAN, *The School for Scandal*

5. But scarce observed, the knowing and the bold
Fall in the general massacre of gold;
Wide-wasting pest! That rages unconfined,
And crowds with crimes the records of mankind;
For gold his sword the hireling ruffian draws,   5
For gold the hireling judge distorts the laws;
Wealth heaped on wealth, nor truth nor safety buys,
The dangers gather as the treasures rise.
—SAMUEL JOHNSON, "The Vanity of Human Wishes"

---

4. Coach to York.

Figurative Language

Figurative language is the inclusive term for words that are used in ways that depart notably from their *literal* applications, so as to achieve special meanings or effects. **Literal language** means what most speakers would perceive as the standard meaning of words, or as their standard order in a sentence. Figurative language is used most often in poetry, but it is essential to all literary genres, in VERSE or prose, as well as to ordinary writing.

Figurative language is usually divided into two broad classes: FIGURES OF THOUGHT and FIGURES OF SPEECH.

FIGURES OF THOUGHT (TROPES)

Figures of thought, or tropes (TRŌPES), are words or phrases used in ways that differ from their standard meaning. One kind of trope compares two very different objects, or transfers qualities of one object to a different object. Such figures of thought include SIMILE, METAPHOR, PERSONIFICATION, and PATHETIC FALLACY. A second kind of trope depends on a contrast between two levels of meaning, or a shift from one level of meaning to another. IRONY is the most widespread example of this type; others are PARADOX, OXYMORON, UNDERSTATEMENT, and HYPERBOLE.

Simile

A **simile** is a FIGURE OF THOUGHT in which one kind of thing is compared to a different object, concept, or experience using the word "like" or "as": "Jen's room is like a pig sty." The simile can also specify some feature of the comparison: "Jen's room is as dirty as a pig sty." In either case, the subject and the analogy are pictured together.

Similes occur in both poetry and prose, and they may be short and simple or long and extended. They provide an important indication of an author or speaker's TONE—that is, implied attitude toward the subject. As with a METAPHOR, the means is to use a comparison that reflects some key quality of the literal subject. For example, the tone of a simile may be exalted, as in Robert Burns's lyrical tribute: "O, my luve's like a red, red rose." Here, the image evoked is of a fresh, vibrant, and lovely object of adoration. The tone may be wry and scornful, as in James Joyce's more extended simile from the SHORT STORY "Two Gallants" describing a self-satisfied loafer: "His head was large, globular and oily; . . . and his large hat, set upon it sideways, looked like a bulb which had grown out of another." The adjective "globular" is extended to the roundness of the double "bulb" of hat and head. The image is ludicrous. It equates the item of clothing with the supposed site of the intellect and also contrasts the man's head with the humble onion to which it is compared.

To take a third example, from *Romeo and Juliet*, the tone may indicate heartbreak, as in Lord Capulet's grief at what he believes is his dead daughter: "Death lies on her like an untimely frost / Upon the sweetest flower of all the field." Here Juliet's death is compared to an early frost that kills a rare and lovely flower. The simile describes the effect of the blighting cold on the frozen but still beautiful plant. It suggests the deathly pallor of the stricken young woman who has so recently looked blushing and vibrant. Although Juliet is not in fact dead at this point, her father's simile on the devastating loss of vitality and hope foreshadows the tragedy to come.

Metaphor   ◄

In a **metaphor**, a word or phrase that in literal use designates one kind of thing is applied to a conspicuously different object, concept, or experience. Unlike a SIMILE, it does not use an explicit comparison. For example, in "Jen's room is a pig sty," the metaphorical word, "sty," is applied to the literal subject, "room," without using "like" or "as." The critic I. A. Richards devised a helpful conception of the metaphorical relationship in *Philosophy of Rhetoric*. He called the literal subject the **tenor**, the aspect that "holds" the meaning, and he termed the analogy the **vehicle**, the part that "conveys" the comparison. In this example, the sty is the vehicle used to convey certain impressions of the room, the tenor. Unlike a SIMILE, in which the tenor and the vehicle are shown side by side, a metaphor describes them as though they were superimposed on each other. It appeals to the reader or listener's imagination by expressing the analogy in terms of sensory impressions. Metaphor is the most comprehensive category of TROPE, or FIGURES OF THOUGHT, all of which use words in ways that depart markedly from their standard literal meanings. (See also SIMILE, PERSONIFICATION, and PATHETIC FALLACY.)

The effect of a metaphor is to transfer to the tenor qualities closely associated with the vehicle. In the simplest metaphors, the analogy may be plain and direct: in the example above, the implication is that Jen's room is dirty and disheveled, as one might expect an enclosure for pigs to be. In more complex metaphors the associations between vehicle and tenor may be intricate and surprising. For example, Romeo, hiding under Juliet's balcony, says, "But soft, what light from yonder window breaks? / It is the east, and Juliet is the sun." The tenor is the light shed by the open window. The vehicle is the brightness and warmth of his young love's beauty, which seem to him as powerful as those of the rising sun. At the same time, the vehicle may convey, subtly, an unexpected and ominous aspect of the tenor. Here, the implication is that Juliet is not literally the solar body but a human being, subject to the forces of time and violence. Romeo's exalted vision suggests how much he ignores or denies as he falls recklessly in love with the daughter of his family's enemy.

A metaphor may be short or long, a quick linking or a series of sustained comparisons. On the simplest level, it is as concise as a single word. That may be a verb (I "wilted," her heart "sang"); an adjective ("leaden" thoughts, a heart "of gold"); or a noun (calling someone an "angel" or a "dragon").

A **mixed metaphor** occurs when two or more conflicting vehicles are applied to the same tenor. Instead of clarifying some aspect of the subject, the figure confuses it by linking images that clash: "She felt a heavy burden of guilt, but she would not let it engulf her determination." The word "burden" is already a vehicle for the tenor, her guilt; it clashes with the second vehicle, "engulf." The image of being weighed down is confused by the conflicting image of being surrounded and swallowed up, drowned. The solution would be to rethink the qualities of the tenor and choose a single vehicle that reflects them: "She felt a heavy burden of guilt, but she would not let it hinder her determination."

Mixed metaphors often occur because the writer is not thinking clearly. In that case, as in the example above, they sound ludicrous. Sometimes, though, authors use them to suggest that a speaker is so carried away by powerful feelings as to be heedless of the mixed vehicles. For instance, Ophelia, distraught over what she believes is Hamlet's sudden plunge into madness, contrasts her distress with the delight of having "sucked the honey of his music vows." The reference to tasting the sweet honey clashes with that of delighting in the musicality of Hamlet's declarations of love. Both, however, express eloquently the young woman's despair over an incalculable loss of something rare and precious. Perhaps the slight unhinging of Ophelia's logic is also meant to foreshadow the complete breakdown of her reason that will shortly follow.

Shakespeare also sometimes uses a series of vehicles for the same tenor in order to suggest how rapidly and desperately a speaker's mind is working. In his expression of total despair, for example, the tyrant Macbeth compares life to "a walking shadow," "a poor player that struts and frets his hour upon the stage," and "a tale told by an idiot." His metaphors convey the sense of transience and futility: the bitter images of meaninglessness. The man who began the play rich in all the worldly blessings has by this point annihilated every person and value he once treasured. In destroying so many other lives, the metaphors imply, he has also destroyed his own.

An **extended metaphor** may also recur through an entire work, and alter or reinforce the depiction of the characters and the plot. For example, the references to gardens in *Hamlet*, to heavenly bodies—stars, sun, moon—in *Romeo and Juliet*, and to birds and flight in *Jane Eyre* gain power and scope from their recurrence and variety.

At whatever level of complexity, a metaphor offers an indirect commentary on the literal action. It is more subtle than simple direct statement because it invites a silent dialogue between author and reader, or reader and speaker. Implication (the author's or speaker's role) and inference (the reader's or listener's response) are the main sources of **subtext**. That is the underlying meaning or set of meanings that provide one of the main challenges and pleasures of literature. Reading for subtext is comparable to having a conversation with a clever, subtle friend. The speaker of Shakespeare's Sonnet 23, a tongue-tied lover, pleads with his love to let his "books" serve as his "eloquence" in expressing his deeply felt thoughts: "O, learn to read what silent love hath writ; / To hear with eyes belongs to love's fine wit." This tribute to the understanding of the perceptive lover might apply as well to the perceptive reader. Metaphor could be called the ultimate expression of "fine wit."

An extended form of personification occurs in **allegory**, in which an abstract concept is presented as though it were a character who speaks and acts as an independent being. In the medieval morality play *Everyman*, for example, the personified characters include not only the hero, Everyman, who represents all human beings as they face death and final judgment, but also such abstract qualities as Beauty, Knowledge, and Good Deeds. The play depicts the extent to which each of these abstractions is able and willing to accompany Everyman on his terrifying final journey toward the grave and the divine reward or punishment beyond it.

Another example of complex allegory is John Bunyan's seventeenth-century work, *The Pilgrim's Progress*; allegoric episodes occur also in many of the novels and short stories of Nathaniel Hawthorne. Jonathan Swift's *Gulliver's Travels* (1726) and George Orwell's *Animal Farm* (1946) use allegory not to glorify a subject but to SATIRIZE it.

Pathetic Fallacy

Pathetic fallacy is a special type of PERSONIFICATION, in which aspects of nature, such as the landscape or the weather, are represented as having human qualities or feelings. The term derives from the logical absurdity ("fallacy") of supposing that nature can sympathize with (feel *pathos* for) human moods and concerns. Usually the pathetic fallacy reflects or foreshadows some aspect of the poem or story at that point, such as the plot, theme, or characterization. The effect is to intensify the tone. For example, a mild, sunny day would promise a tranquil, happy scene, while it is no accident that the dire events in *Hamlet* begin with the ghost's appearance on a winter midnight.

At times, writers reverse the usual use of the pathetic fallacy for purposes of IRONY. For example, the bloody battle of Chancellorville in Stephen Crane's *The Red Badge of Courage* is set on a lovely summer day. On the eve of the battle, the naïve young private Henry Fleming sees nature as attuned to his need for consolation: "There was a caress in the soft winds; and the whole mood of the darkness, he thought, was one of sympathy for himself in his distress." A change in the mood of the weather or the look of the landscape is a favorite means for authors to signal a shift in the fortunes of characters. As Henry encounters the devastation of war, the setting accordingly turns dark and threatening.

EXERCISE: Personification and Pathetic Fallacy

For each of the following passages:

- Specify whether it exemplifies PERSONIFICATION or PATHETIC FALLACY. *Note:* Some excerpts contain more than one FIGURE OF THOUGHT; in those cases, identify both.
- Describe the effects—the impressions and feelings—that result from this use of FIGURATIVE LANGUAGE.

1. *The moment before the protagonist experiences the horror of finding his first decaying corpse, this account of his thoughts occurs:*

   He conceived Nature to be a woman with a deep aversion to tragedy. —STEPHEN CRANE, *The Red Badge of Courage*

2. O Time, thou must untangle this, not I;
   It is too hard a knot for me t'untie.
   —WILLIAM SHAKESPEARE, *Twelfth Night*

3. *Mr. Rochester, who is secretly married to a mad wife whom he cannot legally divorce, proposes bigamous marriage to the unsuspecting Jane Eyre. Just afterwards, the following description occurs:*

   But what had befallen the night? The moon was not yet set, and we were all in shadow: I could scarcely see my master's face, near as I was. And what ailed the chestnut tree? It writhed and groaned; while wind roared in the laurel walk, and came sweeping over us.
   —CHARLOTTE BRONTË, *Jane Eyre*

4. He seemed a part of the mute melancholy landscape, an incarnation of its frozen woe, with all that was warm and sentient in him fast bound below the surface; but there was nothing unfriendly in his silence. I simply felt that he lived in a depth of moral isolation too remote for casual access, and I had the sense that his loneliness was not merely the result of his personal plight, tragic as I guessed that to be, but had in it . . . the profound accumulated cold of many Starkfield[1] winters. —EDITH WHARTON, *Ethan Frome*

---

1. A fictional town in western Massachusetts.

5. *The prince is reflecting on the deaths of the young lovers, who had been caught in the feud between their families:*

A glooming peace this morning with it brings;
The sun for sorrow will not show his head.

—WILLIAM SHAKESPEARE, *Romeo and Juliet*

Irony

Irony is the broadest class of FIGURES OF THOUGHT that depend on presenting a deliberate contrast between two levels of meaning. The major types of irony are VERBAL, STRUCTURAL, DRAMATIC, TRAGIC, and COSMIC.

Verbal irony consists of implying a meaning different from, and often the complete opposite of, the one that is explicitly stated. Usually, the irony is signaled by clues in the situation or in the style of expression. For example, the narrator of Robert Frost's "Provide, Provide," lamenting the transience of fame and power, advises: "Die early, and avoid the fate." The irony is implied by the contrast between the mock wisdom of the tone and the cold comfort of the drastic so-called solution.

In more complex cases, the detection of irony may depend on values that the author assumes are shared by his or her audience. One of the most famous examples is Jonathan Swift's bitter SATIRE "A Modest Proposal." It claims to present a happy solution to the famine in the author's native Ireland: using the infants of the starving lower classes as a source of food. At no point does the narrator abandon his matter-of-fact, complacent tone: the reaction of horror is left to the reader. The risk, which did in fact affect the reception of Swift's essay, is that an audience will mistake irony for serious statement and so miss the underlying meaning altogether. In other words, verbal irony depends on the reader's ability to infer meaning that an author implies, rather than directly expresses. Therefore, irony requires subtle reading comprehension and is always in danger of being misunderstood, and so of shocking or offending a naïve audience.

Sometimes the term **sarcasm**, the taunting use of apparent approval or praise for actual disapproval or dispraise, is mistakenly used as synonymous with "verbal irony." The distinctions are that sarcasm is simpler and more crude; in dialogue, it is often signaled by vocal inflection. For example, someone might react to the news that the car is out of gas with the sarcastic retort, "Great! Just what we needed." In another example, Amanda Wingfield, the controlling mother in Tennessee Williams's play *The Glass Menagerie*, demands to know of her adult son where he has been going at night. Tom, an aspiring writer who feels trapped by having to work in a warehouse to support his mother and sister, has been escaping to bars and movies in his free time. When Amanda calls his explanation that he goes to the movies "a lie," Tom reacts with bitter sarcasm:

> I'm going to opium dens, dens of vice and criminals' hangouts, Mother. I've joined the Hogan Gang, I'm a hired assassin, I carry a tommy gun in a violin case! . . . They call me Killer, Killer Wingfield, I'm leading a double-life, a simple, honest warehouse worker by day, by night a dynamic *czar* of the *underworld*, Mother.

Tom's sarcasm is signaled by the exaggerated details, clichés of gangster movies, which mock Amanda's groundless charges, and by the italicized words that emphasize his frustration and outrage.

Structural irony refers to an implication of alternate or reversed meaning that runs through a work. A major technique for creating structural irony is the use of a naïve protagonist or **unreliable narrator** who continually interprets events and intentions in ways that the author signals are mistaken. For example, Voltaire's Candide, despite several experiences of terrible suffering and corruption, persists in his conviction that "everything is for the best in this best of all possible worlds." Huckleberry Finn, Mark Twain's boy narrator, believes at first that the rascally King and Duke are the brave and learned noblemen they claim to be, despite signs of their shady past and limited education.

Other narrators may be unreliable not because they are naïve but because they are mentally deficient. The narrator of Edgar Allan Poe's short story "The Tell-Tale Heart" is paranoid and hallucinatory. He claims that his extraordinarily acute senses and clear motives for murdering an old man—the victim has regarded him with a filmy and thus, he asserts, evil eye—are proofs that he is "not mad." A reader who accepts this self-defense at face value is missing the story's well-sustained structural irony.

Dramatic irony occurs when the audience has knowledge that one or more of the characters lacks. The technique may be used for comic or tragic effects. In *Twelfth Night* Shakespeare lets us in from the first scene on the secret that Viola is disguised as a boy and that she is in love with the duke whom she is serving as page. We can therefore enjoy the humorous dramatic ironies that result when the Countess Olivia, the object of the duke's courtship, falls in love with the charming messenger. In Homer's *Odyssey*, the long-absent Odysseus's disguise as a beggar provides poignant dramatic irony. As he encounters various beloved family members and hated rivals, he must, for the sake of his intended revenge, refrain from revealing his true identity. The audience is flattered by being allowed to share in the OMNISCIENT POINT OF VIEW often reserved for the author.

When dramatic irony occurs in tragedies, it is called **tragic irony**. For example, the audience knows from the opening scene of *Othello* that the epithet "honest Iago" is IRONIC. While pretending to serve the noble general faithfully, Iago is plotting his downfall. In *Oedipus Rex*, Oedipus searches for the murderer of King Laius. He discovers that the culprit is himself, and that the king was his father and the widowed queen, whom he has married, his own mother. In *Romeo and Juliet*, Mercutio misunderstands his friend Romeo's motives for refusing to respond to Tybalt's challenge. Unlike Mercutio, we know that Romeo is secretly married to Juliet, the daughter of his family's enemy. Rather than acting out of fear, he is trying to avoid conflict with Tybalt, who has just become his cousin by marriage. Mercutio takes Romeo's courtesy for cowardice and unintentionally triggers the series of deaths that devastate both families.

Cosmic irony refers to an implied worldview in which characters are led to embrace false hopes of aid or success, only to be defeated by some larger force, such as God or fate. For instance, Macbeth believes that he is protected by the weird sisters' prophecies, but he is betrayed by their fiendish duplicity. Arthur Miller's Willy Loman kills himself to secure his family the insurance payment that his suicide will, in fact, make invalid. Shakespeare's *King Lear* is a tour de force of cosmic irony, in which several characters congratulate themselves on a triumph or a narrow escape, only to be destroyed shortly afterward.

The presentation of complex, even contradictory, attitudes toward experience, and the interpretation of possible motives or outcomes in more than one way, are major sources of literature's richness. Because life itself is full of contradictions and unexpected turns, irony has long had a special appeal to writers and readers alike.

EXERCISE: Irony

For each of the following examples:

- Identify the IRONY as VERBAL, STRUCTURAL, DRAMATIC, TRAGIC, or COSMIC.
- Explain why that type of IRONY applies to the example.
- Describe the effects—the impressions and feelings—created by the IRONY.

1. She thinks that even up in heaven
       Her class lies late and snores,
    While poor black cherubs rise at seven
       To do celestial chores.

    —COUNTEE CULLEN, "For a Lady I Know"

2. *In Shakespeare's* King Lear, *Edmund, the illegitimate son of the Earl of Gloucester, falsely accuses his brother, Edgar, of plotting their father's death. The gullible Earl, believing his treacherous son, calls Edgar a "villain" and Edmund a "loyal and natural boy." He gives orders to have Edgar killed and promises to transfer Edgar's entire inheritance to Edmund.*

3. *In Robert Browning's "Porphyria's Lover," the narrator describes his solution to the social barriers that separate him from his wealthy lady love: when she comes to his lonely chamber, he strangles her with her long yellow hair. The poem concludes:*

    I propped her head up as before,
       Only, this time my shoulder bore
    Her head, which droops upon it still:
       The smiling, rosy little head,
    So glad it has its utmost will,   5
       That all it scorned at once is fled,
       And I, its love, am gained instead!
    Porphyria's love: she guessed not how
       Her darling one wish would be heard.
    And thus we sit together now,   10
       And all night long we have not stirred,
       And yet God has not said a word!

4. *In Shakespeare's* Henry V, *the night before the battle of Agincourt, the king disguises himself as one of his own officers and visits his troops, attempting to raise their spirits. He assures some soldiers that he is prepared to fight selflessly in support of King Henry's causes:*

    Methinks I could not die anywhere so contented as in the king's company.

5. *In Mark Twain's* Adventures of Huckleberry Finn, *the narrator, a poor Southern boy living in the days before emancipation, has helped a runaway slave to escape. Huck has acted impulsively, out of compassion for the slave, Jim, but he knows that his actions go against the dictates of his society's legal system and customs. He decides to "do the right thing and the clean thing" and return Jim to his owner. After he has written the telltale letter, he starts reminiscing about their long raft trip down the Mississippi and recalls how Jim "would always . . . do everything he could think of for me, and how good he always was." Huck looks at the letter and says: "I was a trembling, because I'd got to decide, forever, betwixt two things, and I knowed it. I studied a minute, sort of holding my breath, and then says to myself: 'All right, then, I'll go to hell'—and tore it up."*

6. *In Shakespeare's* A Midsummer Night's Dream, *the fairy queen, Titania, is given a drug by her mischievous husband, Oberon, the fairy king, that causes her to fall in love with the next creature that she sees. That happens to be the coarse Athenian workman, Nick Bottom, whom Oberon has magically transformed into an ass. Gazing starry-eyed at her hairy new love, Titania murmurs, "Thou art as wise as thou art beautiful."*

7. *In Shakespeare's* Macbeth, *Macduff, the nobleman whose entire family the king has had murdered, challenges Macbeth to a duel. He responds scornfully with the prophecy that three witches have told him: "I bear a charmed life which must not yield / To one of woman born." Macduff responds with the revelation that he was born by Caesarian section:*

> Despair thy charm
> And let the angel whom thou still hast served
> Tell thee, Macduff was from his mother's womb
> Untimely ripped.

TROPES DEPENDENT ON CONTRASTING LEVELS OF MEANING

In addition to IRONY, a number of other TROPES depend on contrasts in levels of meaning: HYPERBOLE, UNDERSTATEMENT, PARADOX, OXYMORON, and PUN. Such FIGURES OF THOUGHT may or may not be IRONIC. The test is whether or not the speaker intends to imply an underlying meaning that differs from the literal one.

Hyperbole ◀

Hyperbole (hi-PER-boh-lee) is a TROPE in which a point is stated in a way that is greatly exaggerated. The effect of hyperbole is often to imply the intensity of a speaker's feelings or convictions by putting them in overstated or absolute terms. In this way, it is the opposite of UNDERSTATEMENT. For example, in John Donne's "The Sun Rising," the speaker declares of himself and his lover: "She's all states, and all princes, I, / Nothing else is." The **hyperbolic** claim suggests the passionate lover's self-assurance and egotism.

Hyperbole may be comic, as in the tall tales of the American West, or serious, as in cases where the excessive feeling signals an ominous imbalance. For example, Othello, greeting his new wife after surviving a perilous storm, says:

> O my soul's joy!
> If after every tempest come such calms,
> May the winds blow till they have wakened death!

He means only to show his overwhelming elation and relief. The hyperbole also foreshadows, however, the loss of control that will later lead Othello to act on his violent feelings to the point that they do indeed "waken[ ] death" for his beloved and himself.

Understatement ◀

Understatement is a form of IRONY in which a point is deliberately expressed as less, in extent, value, or importance, than it actually is. For example, in *Romeo and Juliet*, Mercutio dismisses the fatal wound he has just received as "a scratch." He elaborates on the figure with a second understatement: "Marry, 'tis enough." The effect is to create a sort of double take. The force of the implied meaning—here, that Mercutio is well aware that he has suffered a death blow—is intensified by the restraint with which it is expressed. In this sense, the TROPE is the opposite of HYPERBOLE, in which an attitude or feeling is greatly exaggerated.

Understatement may also be used for comic or SATIRIC effect. For example, Jonathan Swift's ESSAY describing a grotesque plan for relieving starvation in his native Ireland by using the babies of the poor as food has the seemingly bland title "A Modest Proposal."

In more recent times, such writers as Franz Kafka, Ernest Hemingway, and Raymond Carver have made highly effective use of understatement. For example, in Hemingway's story "The Kill-

ers," two gangsters come into the diner where the teenaged protagonist, Nick Adams, works. They boast that they have been hired
to kill a prizefighter who has apparently reneged on a deal with the
mob. Meanwhile, they callously eat dinner and amuse themselves
by threatening Nick and his coworkers. When the boxer does not
arrive, the killers go off to find him. At his boss George's suggestion, Nick bravely goes to the boxer's rooming house to warn him of
his danger. He finds that the man, who is kind and humble, is well
aware of the situation and convinced that he is doomed. Staring at
the wall and talking in "the same flat voice" throughout, he refuses
all of Nick's well-intended assurances and thanks him for coming.

Nick, horrified, returns to the diner and tells his boss how he
feels: "I can't stand to think about him waiting in the room and
knowing he's going to get it. It's too damned awful." Nick's pity and
frustration are evident in his fervent declarations. George, older
and more resigned, gives a matter-of-fact, understated reply that
pointedly ignores Nick's anguish: "'Well,' said George, 'you better
not think about it.'" The story ends with that understatement. The
effect is to intensify the shock over the ruthless violence to come by
implying that even good men are powerless to stop it.

Paradox

Paradox is a TROPE in which a statement that appears on the surface to be contradictory or impossible turns out to express an often
striking truth. For example, the **paradoxical** slogan of the Bauhaus
School of art and architecture is "Less is more." It suggests that
spareness and selectivity are more important in achieving artistic
beauty than range and inclusiveness. Emily Dickinson's poem "Success Is Counted Sweetest" uses a paradox in finishing that thought:
"Success is counted sweetest / By those who ne'er succeed." The
lines mean that those who most highly value success are, in seeming contradiction to logic, the very ones who have never experi-
enced it. The adjective "sweetest" is a metaphor that implies how
delicious the "taste" of such achievement seems to those who can
only imagine it.

Oxymoron ◀

An **oxymoron** (ox-ih-MOR-on) is a compressed PARADOX. It closely links two seemingly contradictory elements in a way that, on further consideration, turns out to make good sense. Common examples of the TROPE are "bittersweet," "a living death," and "passive aggressive." As with paradox, the effect is to suggest a subtle truth. In the last expression, for example, the oxymoron implies that refusal to take action can be a means of asserting one's will.

Often in literature an oxymoron is a sign of a speaker's conflicted feelings. For example, when Juliet discovers that her new husband has just slain her cousin Tybalt, she exclaims: "O serpent heart, hid with a flowering face! . . . / Beautiful tyrant! fiend angelical!" Juliet is outraged at the seeming conflict between Romeo's physical beauty and the moral corruption that she thinks is revealed by his violent act.

Oxymorons can also create humor by exposing a speaker's confusion. In Shakespeare's *A Midsummer Night's Dream*, for example, Duke Theseus mocks the ridiculous description of the play that some plodding Athenian workmen propose to present to his court: "Merry and tragical? Tedious and brief? / That is hot ice and wondrous strange snow. / How shall we find the concord of this discord?" The clever nobleman is signaling his delight at the absurd contradictions by describing them with equally silly oxymorons.

Pun ◀

A **pun** is a FIGURE OF THOUGHT that plays on words that have the same sound (homonyms), or closely similar sounds, but have sharply contrasted meanings. The usual effect is a witty or humorous double meaning. For example, Shakespeare was fond of punning on "Will," which was not only his nickname, but in his day meant "desire," especially "carnal desire"; see his Sonnets 135 and 136. Puns were especially popular in Renaissance and metaphysical literature, written in the late sixteenth and early seventeenth centuries. They have also been used extensively by such modern writers as James Joyce, Samuel Beckett, and Tom Stoppard.

Although the usual tone of puns is humorous, they can also have a serious intent. For example, in *Hamlet*, the prince's despised uncle makes a public inquiry about his continued depression—"How is it the clouds still hang on you?" Hamlet answers with a pun: "Not

▼

so, my lord. I am too much in the sun." The retort is a reminder to the listening court and to Claudius, who has succeeded Hamlet's father on the throne, of two points: that the prince both dislikes this light of royal favor being shone on him ("sun") and that he feels too strongly his father's loss (as his "son") to celebrate Claudius's kingship. The pun is both clever and ominous. It announces the prince's instinctive loathing for the man whom he will soon discover has murdered his father. It also suggests the roundabout, intellectual nature of Hamlet's weapon of choice, "words, words, words."

EXERCISE: Tropes Dependent on Contrasting Levels of Meaning

For each of the following passages:

- Name the TROPE—HYPERBOLE, UNDERSTATEMENT, PARADOX, OXYMORON, or PUN. *Note:* Some passages may exemplify more than one form.
- Explain why that term applies.
- Describe the effects—the impressions and feelings—created by the contrasts in levels of meaning.

1. *The following dialogue takes place between Henry V and Catherine, the French princess he is courting, whose grasp of English is uncertain:*

   KING HENRY Do you like me, Kate?
   CATHERINE Pardonnez-moi, I cannot tell what is "like me."
   KING HENRY An angel is like you, Kate, and you are like an angel.
   —WILLIAM SHAKESPEARE, *Henry V*

2. It is in giving that we receive;
   It is in pardoning that we are pardoned.
   —Prayer of St. Francis of Assisi

3. The stars are not wanted now: put out every one;
   Pack up the moon and dismantle the sun;
   Pour away the ocean and sweep up the wood;
   For nothing now can ever come to any good.
   —W. H. AUDEN, "Funeral Blues"

4. *Hamlet, having mistakenly killed an interfering old courtier in the act of spying for the king, addresses the body:*

   Take thy fortune.
   Thou find'st to be too busy is some danger.
   —WILLIAM SHAKESPEARE, *Hamlet*

5. *Romeo reacts to the news that, for the crime of slaying Tybalt, he has been banished from Verona, where his new wife, Juliet, resides:*

There is no world without Verona walls,
But purgatory, torture, hell itself.
—WILLIAM SHAKESPEARE, *Romeo and Juliet*

6. *Romeo, dejected by his unrequited infatuation for Rosaline, gives this description of love:*

Feather of lead, bright smoke, cold fire, sick health,
Still-waking sleep, that is not what it is!
—WILLIAM SHAKESPEARE, *Romeo and Juliet*

FIGURES OF SPEECH (SCHEMES)

Figures of speech, also called **schemes**, depend upon a change in the standard order or usual SYNTAX of words to create special effects. The term "figures of speech" is sometimes used to refer to the much broader category of TROPES, which depend on changes not in the order or SYNTAX but in the standard meanings of words. More specifically, however, it describes a smaller category of terms, including APOSTROPHE, RHETORICAL QUESTION, and ANAPHORA.

Apostrophe ◀

An **apostrophe** (a-POS-troh-fee) is an address to a dead or absent person or to an inanimate object or abstract idea. The aim is not, of course, to evoke a response—that would be impossible—but to elevate the style or to create strong emotion. For example, Wordsworth's sonnet, "London, 1802," begins with an apostrophe to the long-dead poet John Milton: "Milton! thou shouldst be living at this hour: / England hath need of thee." In Shakespeare's *Romeo and Juliet*, the young heroine, awaiting her honeymoon with Romeo, **apostrophizes** a personification of night to guide her through the thrilling and intimidating experience: "Come, civil night, / Thou sober-suited matron all in black, / And learn me how to lose a winning match, / Played for a pair of stainless maidenhoods."

In *A Midsummer Night's Dream*, Shakespeare makes fun of the usual serious use of apostrophe in his comic play-within-the-play, "Pyramus and Thisbe." The dim-witted Athenian workmen who perform it have a literal-minded conception of the stage set. They cast members of their company to represent the Wall that separates the lovers and the Moon that shines on their meeting. In one hilarious moment, Bottom, playing Pyramus, pleads: "Thou wall, O wall, O sweet and lovely wall, / Show me thy chink, to blink through with mine eyne." In contrast to the usual absence of a response in an apostrophe, the Wall "*holds up his fingers.*"

A special form of apostrophe is the **invocation**, in which the poet addresses an appeal to a muse or a god to provide inspiration. Such epic poems as Homer's *Odyssey* begin with an invocation: "Sing in me, Muse, and through me tell the story / of that man skilled in all ways of contending."[1]

Rhetorical Question

A **rhetorical question** is a FIGURE OF SPEECH in which a question is posed not to evoke a reply but to emphasize a clearly implied conclusion. The goal is to create a stronger effect than might be achieved by a direct statement. An everyday example is: "Can you imagine that?" The point is to stress that a surprising or shocking thing has in fact happened. A less courteous example from ordinary conversation—"Are you crazy?"—is meant to imply that the person addressed is behaving strangely.

In Wilfred Owen's "Futility," the narrator, seeing the body of a young soldier who has been killed in the First World War, asks the heart-wrenching rhetorical question: "Was it for this the clay grew tall?" William Blake's "Holy Thursday (II)" is a bitter denouncement of the suffering of poor children in the charity schools of eighteenth-century England. The narrator expresses his outrage in a series of rhetorical questions:

> Is this a holy thing to see
> In a rich and fruitful land,
> Babes reduced to misery,
> Fed with cold and usurous hand?
>
> Is that trembling cry a song?
> Can it be a song of joy?
> And so many children poor?

---

1. Trans. Robert Fitzgerald (New York: Farrar, Straus and Giroux, 1998), p. 1.

Anaphora ◄

Anaphora (a-NAF-or-ah) is the intentional repetition of words or phrases at the beginning of successive lines, stanzas, sentences, or paragraphs. It is used frequently in both poetry and prose to create emphasis. Anaphora occurs often in both the Old and New Testaments. A prominent example is the series of Beatitudes ("blessings" promised the faithful) from Jesus's Sermon on the Mount, all of which begin with the phrase "blessed are the . . . ": "Blessed are the merciful, for they shall obtain mercy, / Blessed are the pure in heart, for they shall see God" (Matthew 5.7–8). African American spirituals, inspired by biblical sources, often use anaphora, as in "Go Down, Moses," with its poignant refrain, "Let my people go."

Walt Whitman's "Song of Myself" is full of anaphora. One example is the narrator's response to a child's question—"What is the grass?" He gives a series of whimsical answers, all of which contain the phrase "I guess": "I guess it must be the flag of my disposition, out of hopeful green stuff woven. / Or I guess it is the handkerchief of the Lord." The effect is a soothing, rhythmic harmony. In contrast, in "The Charge of the Light Brigade," Tennyson uses anaphora to suggest the speed and tension of a fatal battle: "Cannon to right of them, / Cannon to left of them, / Cannon in front of them / Volleyed and thundered."

EXERCISE: Figures of Speech (Schemes)

For each of the following passages:

- Identify the FIGURE OF SPEECH: APOSTROPHE, RHETORICAL QUESTION, or ANAPHORA. *Note:* Some passages may contain more than one *figure of speech.*
- Explain why that term applies.
- Describe the effects—the impressions and feelings—created by the FIGURE OF SPEECH.

1. Bring me my Bow of burning gold:
    Bring me my Arrows of desire:
    Bring me my Spear: O clouds unfold!
    Bring me my Chariot of fire!
    –WILLIAM BLAKE, "And Did Those Feet"

2. Bright star, would I were steadfast as thou art—
    –JOHN KEATS, "Bright Star"

3. *In Shakespeare's* Hamlet, *Laertes returns from France to discover that his beloved sister, Ophelia, has gone mad with grief over the murder of their father. As he watches her insane antics, he utters the following cry:*

    Do you see this, O God?

4. I have a dream that one day this nation will rise up and live out the true meaning of its creed: 'We hold these truths to be self-evident: that all men are created equal.' I have a dream that one day on the red hills of Georgia the sons of former slaves and the sons of former slave owners will be able to sit down together at a table of brotherhood. . . . I have a dream that my four children will one day live in a nation where they will not be judged by the color of their skin but by the content of their character.

    –MARTIN LUTHER KING, JR., Speech delivered at
    the Lincoln Memorial, August 28, 1963

5. *In James Joyce's "Counterparts," a domineering boss confronts an employee who denies knowing the whereabouts of some missing papers.*

    "You—*know*—*nothing.* Of course you know nothing," said Mr. Alleyne. "Tell me," he added, glancing first for approval to the lady beside him, "do you take me for a fool? Do you think me an utter fool?"

Rhetorical Strategies

Rhetorical strategy is a loose term for techniques that help to shape or enhance a literary work. Some rhetorical strategies involve DICTION, the level of abstraction and formality of the word choice. Others, such as ALLUSION, describe a reference to some element outside of the work. Some rhetorical strategies concern a pattern that influences a work's TONE—for example, its IMAGERY, SYMBOLISM, and ATMOSPHERE. Still others, such as the REPETITION of ideas and the SELECTION AND ORDER OF DETAILS, describe aspects of the work's content and organization.

Diction ◀

Diction means the word choice and phrasing in a literary work. Diction may be described in terms of various qualities, such as the degree to which it is formal or colloquial, abstract or concrete, LITERAL or FIGURATIVE, or whether it is derived largely from Latin or from Anglo-Saxon. For example, the following passage from *Rambler* No. 5, an essay by the eighteenth-century man of letters Samuel Johnson, describes the optimism that each new springtime evoked in an acquaintance. It is written in **formal**, learned diction:

> The spring, indeed, did often come without any of those effects, but he was always certain that the next would be more propitious; nor was ever convinced that the present spring would fail him before the middle of summer; for he always talked of the spring as coming till it was past, and when it was once past, everyone agreed with him that it was coming.
>
> By long converse with this man, I am, perhaps, brought to feel immoderate pleasure in the contemplation of this delightful season; but I have the satisfaction of finding many, whom it can be no shame to resemble, infected with the same enthusiasm; for there is, I believe, scarce any poet of eminence, who has not left some testimony of his fondness for the flowers, the zephyrs, and the warblers of the spring. Nor has the most luxuriant imagination been able to describe the serenity and happiness of the golden age, otherwise than by gaining a perpetual spring, as the highest reward of uncorrupted innocence.

The passage contains several characteristics of formal diction. The sentences are lengthy and COMPLEX, full of subordinate clauses. The vocabulary is typically Latinate, Johnson preferring "propitious" and "converse" to the Anglo-Saxon "lucky" and "talk." The use of round-about expressions ("zephyrs" and "warblers" rather than the more straightforward "warm winds" and "songbirds") also elevates the diction. The formal, assured diction creates an air of authority fitting for the moralist who is the implied writer of the essay.

In contrast, the American novelist and short story writer Ernest Hemingway made a point of writing in **colloquial**—informal—diction. The following description of a trip to Spain is from his novel *The Sun Also Rises* (1925):

> The bus climbed steadily up the road. The country was barren and rocks stuck up through the clay. There was no grass beside the road. Looking back we could see the country spread out below. Far back the fields were squares of green and brown on the hillsides. Making the horizon were the brown mountains. They were strangely shaped. As we climbed higher the horizon kept changing. As the bus ground slowly up the road we could see other mountains coming up in the south. Then the road came over the crest, flattened out, and went into a forest. It was a forest of cork trees, and the sun came through the trees in patches, and there were cattle grazing back in the trees. We went through the forest and the road came out and turned along a rise of land, and out ahead of us was a rolling green plain, with dark mountains beyond it. These were not like the brown, heat-baked mountains we had left behind. These were wooded and there were clouds coming down from them. The green plain stretched off.

Several qualities convey the colloquial level of the diction. The SYN-TAX is plain, containing either short, SIMPLE sentences or COMPOUND sentences made up of clauses linked by "and." The vocabulary is Anglo-Saxon, and it is based on simple nouns, such as "rocks," "squares," and "trees." Several words and phrases are repeated: "green," "brown," "mountains," and "These were." The style creates an impression of frankness and objectivity. The narrator seems in tight control of his feelings, observant of the landscape but determined not to seem sentimental or overly emotional.

A writer's diction may also differ enormously in its relative levels of **abstraction**—that is, the extent to which it deals with general concepts. The opposite quality is **concreteness**: references to physical objects, IMAGERY, and details about the feelings and the senses. For example, "love," "patriotism," "beauty," and "time" are **abstract** terms, while "lips," "gun," "silky gown," and "shrill cry" are concrete. Most literary works contain both abstract and concrete diction, in varying degrees. Often a writer will illustrate an abstract concept with concrete details. For example, in John Keats's "Ode to a Nightingale," the narrator describes with increasingly concrete diction a magical wine that could make him oblivious to life's sufferings:

> O, for a draught of vintage! That hath been
> Cooled a long age in the deep-delvèd earth,
> Tasting of Flora[1] and the country green,
> Dance, and Provençal song,[2] and sunburnt mirth!
> O for a beaker full of the warm South,
> Full of the true, the blushful Hippocrene,[3]
>   With beaded bubbles winking at the brim,
>   And purple-stainèd mouth.

The passage moves from a description of a "vintage" whose taste involves such abstractions as "Flora," "the country green," and "dance" to the more specific sensations of the sound of "Provençal song" and the look and feel of "sunburnt mirth." It builds to the concrete details of the "blushful" look of the wine in a glass, its "beaded bubbles winking at the brim," leaving the happy drinker with "purple-stainèd mouth."

A writer might also imply an abstract concept or theme, which must be inferred from a series of concrete descriptions or images. Christina Rossetti's "Goblin Market" is a poem about the dangers of giving way to pleasurable but fatal temptations. Rossetti gives that THEME concrete form by depicting it as forbidden fruits sold by goblins, who use them to ensnare the souls of innocent maidens. The evil nature of the "little men" is suggested by the concrete details describing their physical appearance, all features of lowly animals:

> One had a cat's face,
> One whisked a tail,
> One tramped at a rat's pace,
> One crawled like a snail.

The afflicted maiden implies how addictive the goblins' wares are as she recalls the temperature, texture, look, and taste of the fruit that she longs to eat again:

> "What melons icy-cold
> Piled on a dish of gold

---

1. Roman goddess of spring.
2. Of medieval troubadours from southern France.
3. Fountain of the Greek muses.

Too huge for me to hold,
What peaches with a velvet nap,
Pellucid grapes without one seed;
Odorous indeed must be the mead
Whereon they grow, and pure the wave they drink
With lilies at the brink,
And sugar-sweet their sap."

The aptness of a particular level of diction depends partly on
the context in which it is being used. For example, a philosophical
essay would tend to use words that are formal, often Latinate,
and abstract, while a LYRIC poem would likely be more COLLOQUIAL
and concrete. For those generalizations, too, however, there are
exceptions. For example, Tennyson, a poet whose work is full of
sensuous details and images, also uses abstract diction at times
with great effectiveness. In "Ulysses," he imagines the Greek hero
Odysseus, whom he calls by his Latin name, in old age. He is frus-
trated by inaction and rallying his "mariners" for one last adventure.
Ulysses speaks in a series of abstract concepts:

Though much is taken, much abides; and though
We are not now that strength which in old days
Moved earth and heaven, that which we are, we are—
One equal temper of heroic hearts,
Made weak by time and fate, but strong in will
To strive, to seek, to find, and not to yield.

The abstractions express both the virtues that the men have brought
to their previous triumphs—"strength" and "heroic hearts"—and the
enormous forces—"time" and "fate"—that Ulysses knows will inevitably defeat them. Still, he urges them to continue to "strive . . . and
not to yield," so that they may go out in a moment of glory. A concrete description of a specific venture might have exposed the physical limitations and perhaps the hubris of the old hero. The soaring
abstractions, however, elevate his doomed quest and reflect Ulysses's
unflinching valor. A work's diction, then, should reflect the writer's
meaning and TONE and suit the intended audience.

Allusion ◄

An **allusion** (al-LOO-zyun) is a passing reference in a work of literature to another literary or historical work, figure, or event, or to a literary passage. The reference is not explained, so that it can convey the flattering assumption that the reader shares the writer's learning or inside knowledge. For example, in Andrea Lee's novel *Sarah Phillips* (1984), the narrator describes her Harvard roommate, a chemistry major and "avid lacrosse player" who "adored fresh air and loathed reticence and ambiguity," as having the following surprising preference: "Margaret, the scientist, had . . . a positively Brontëesque conception of the ideal man." The allusion is to the dark, brooding, mysterious heroes in the works of Charlotte and Emily Brontë, especially Mr. Rochester in *Jane Eyre* and Heathcliff in *Wuthering Heights*. Only a reader who recognizes the allusion would appreciate the IRONY of the frank, forthright Margaret's attraction to men who are far from being either frank or forthright.

The title of William Faulkner's *The Sound and the Fury* (1929) presents a more complex example. It **alludes** to the SOLILOQUY in Shakespeare's *Macbeth* in which the embittered PROTAGONIST dismisses all of life as merely "a tale / Told by an idiot, full of sound and fury, / Signifying nothing." The aptness of the reference becomes evident when the reader discovers that the first part of the novel is told from the perspective of a mentally challenged narrator, who is incapable of meaningful speech. Thus, an allusion can provide a rich network of associations and intensify the effects of a passage or a whole work.

In other situations, in which the subject is weak or unimportant when compared to the literary or historical source, an allusion may create a sense of IRONIC deflation. T. S. Eliot calls attention to that use of the technique in "The Love Song of J. Alfred Prufrock." The insecure narrator, feeling hopelessly inadequate in polite society, says of his efforts to court women:

> . . . though I have wept and fasted, wept and prayed,
> Though I have seen my head (grown slightly bald) brought in
>   upon a platter,
> I am no prophet—and here's no great matter. . . .

The allusion is to John the Baptist, the prophet in the New Testament who was beheaded after he refused to compromise his moral principles by giving in to the seductress Salome. Prufrock envisions his own severed head, made ludicrous by its balding state, exposed to public scrutiny and his earnest courtship amounting to "no great matter."

▼

EXERCISES: Allusion and Diction

I. For each of the following passages:
*   Identify the ALLUSION.
*   Explain how that term applies.
*   Describe the effects of this RHETORICAL STRATEGY on the meaning and the tone of the passage.

1. *For his fourteenth birthday, the protagonist of Jhumpa Lahiri's* The Namesake, *Gogol Ganguli, whose parents are from India, received a gift from his father. It is a book of short stories by the Russian writer for whom he was named:*

> At the door [his father] pauses, turns around. "Do you know what Dostoyevsky once said?"
> Gogol shakes his head.
> "'We all came out of Gogol's overcoat.'"
> "What's that supposed to mean?"
> "It will make sense to you one day. Many happy returns of the day."
> Gogol gets up and shuts the door behind his father, who has the annoying habit of always leaving it partly open. He fastens the lock on the knob for good measure, then wedges the book on a high shelf between two volumes of the Hardy Boys. He settles down again with his lyrics on the bed when something occurs to him. This writer he is named after—Gogol isn't his first name. His first name is Nikolai. Not only does Gogol Ganguli have a pet name turned good name, but a last name turned first name. And so it occurs to him that no one he knows in the world, in Russia or India or America or anywhere, shares his name. Not even the source of his namesake.

2. *The narrator of the following passage is recalling an encounter that took place when she was ten years old:*

> . . . when I saw him lift and poise the book and stand in act to hurl it, I instinctively started aside with a cry of alarm: not soon enough, however; the volume was flung, it hit me, and I fell, striking my head against the door and cutting it. The cut bled, the pain was sharp: my terror had passed its climax; other feelings succeeded.
> "Wicked and cruel boy!" I said. "You are like a murderer—you are like a slave driver—you are like the Roman emperors!"
> I had read Goldsmith's "History of Rome," and had formed my opinion of Nero, Caligula, &c. Also I had drawn parallels in silence, which I never thought thus to have declared aloud.
> —CHARLOTTE BRONTÉ, *Jane Eyre*

II. For each of the following passages:
*   Identify the level and generality of the DICTION: FORMAL or COLLOQUIAL; ABSTRACT or CONCRETE. Note that some passages may exemplify more than one kind of DICTION.
*   Explain why the term or terms apply.
*   Describe the effects of the DICTION on the meaning and TONE.

1. The old lady settled herself comfortably, removing her white cotton gloves and putting them up with her purse on the shelf in front of the back window. The children's mother still had on slacks and still had her head tied up in a green kerchief, but the grandmother had on a navy blue sailor hat with a bunch of white violets on the brim and a navy blue dress with a small white dot in the print. Her collar and cuffs were white organdy trimmed with lace and at her neckline she had pinned a spray of cloth violets containing a sachet. In case of an accident anyone seeing her dead on the highway would know at once that she was a lady.
    –FLANNERY O'CONNOR, "A Good Man Is Hard to Find"

2. The instructor said,
    > Go home and write
    > a page tonight.
    > And let that page come out of you—
    > Then, it will be true.   5

    I wonder if it's that simple?
    I am twenty-two, colored, born in Winston-Salem.
    I went to school there, then Durham, then here
    to this college on the hill above Harlem.
    I am the only colored student in my class.   10
    The steps from the hill lead down into Harlem,
    through a park, then I cross St. Nicholas,
    Eighth Avenue, Seventh, and I come to the Y,
    the Harlem Branch Y, where I take the elevator
    up to my room, sit down, and write this page.   15
    –LANGSTON HUGHES, "Theme for English B"

3. Trust thyself: every heart vibrates to that iron string. Accept the place the divine Providence has found for you; the society of your contemporaries, the connexion of events. Great men have always done so and confided themselves childlike to the genius of their age, betraying their perception that the Eternal was stirring at their heart, working through their hands, predominating in all their being. And we are now men, and must accept in the highest mind

▼

the same transcendent destiny; and not pinched in a corner, not cowards fleeing before a revolution, but redeemers and benefactors, pious aspirants to be noble clay plastic[1] under the Almighty effort, let us advance on Chaos and the Dark.

–RALPH WALDO EMERSON, "Self-Reliance"

4. In the hickory scent
   Among slabs of pork
   Glistening with salt,
   I played Indian
   In a headdress of redbird feathers   5
   & brass buttons
   Off my mother's winter coat.
   Smoke wove
   A thread of fire through meat, into December
   & January. The dead weight   10
   Of the place hung around me,
   Strung up with sweetgrass.   –YUSEF KOMUNYAKAA, "The Smokehouse"

►
Imagery

Imagery is a widely used term that has several distinctive meanings. All, however, refer to the CONCRETE, rather than the ABSTRACT, aspects of a literary work.

In a narrow sense, imagery means a visual description of an object or a scene—an **image** or picture of it, especially one that is detailed and vivid. The opening stanza of Algernon Charles Swinburne's "The Forsaken Garden" fits that definition:

In a coign[2] of the cliff between lowland and highland,
    At the sea-down's edge between windward and lee,
Walled round with rocks as an inland island,
    The ghost of a garden fronts the sea.
A girdle of brushwood and thorn encloses
    The steep square slope of the blossomless bed
Where the weeds that grew green from the graves of its roses
    Now lie dead.

Swinburne's details about the location, landmarks, and foliage create a vivid verbal sketch of the "forsaken" spot, an "inland island"

---

1. Malleable.
2. Corner.

formed by a rock wall on the "steep . . . slope" of a cliff. It is so barren that not only the "roses" but even the "weeds" that once lived on the flowers' "graves" have died. Only "brushwood" and "thorn" now grow in the "ghost of a garden."

The broad meaning of imagery, however, includes all the references to sensory perception that a work contains or evokes. Those include not only the objects, actions, and scenes depicted in literal descriptions, but also in ALLUSIONS and in the VEHICLES of METAPHORS and SIMILES. Moreover, in this broad sense, the term is not limited to the appeals to sight, but also includes descriptions and evocations of sound, touch, taste, smell, temperature, and movement.

For example, Li-Young Lee's "Persimmons" uses vivid imagery in this broader sense to describe the narrator's experience of visiting his elderly father, a painter who has gone blind:*

This year, in the muddy lighting
of my parents' cellar, I rummage, looking
for something I lost.
My father sits on the tired, wooden stairs,
black cane between his knees,
hand over hand, gripping the handle.
He's so happy that I've come home.
I ask how his eyes are, a stupid question.
All gone, he answers.

Under some blankets, I find a box.
Inside the box I find three scrolls.
I sit beside him and untie
three paintings by my father:
Hibiscus leaf and a white flower.
Two cats preening.
Two persimmons, so full they want to drop from the cloth.

He raises both hands to touch the cloth,
asks, *Which is this?*

This is persimmons, Father.

Oh, the feel of the wolftail on the silk,
the strength, the tense
precision in the wrist.
I painted them hundreds of times
eyes closed. These I painted blind.

---

*This excerpt from "Persimmons" is reprinted with the permission of BOA Editions.

▼

sey, *Adventures of Huckleberry Finn*, and *Heart of Darkness*. In other works, beginning with the Book of Genesis in the Hebrew Bible, the snake is a symbol of enticing but dangerous temptation. In many literary works, however, a symbol is unique in that its meaning is particular to that poem, play, or story and must be inferred by the reader as the work develops.

In the last case, a symbol differs from an ALLEGORY, a sustained and limited analogy between a subject and an image to which it is compared. A symbol is both more complex and less specific. For example, Nathaniel Hawthorne's "Young Goodman Brown" is an allegory in which a young Puritan ignores the warning of his wife, who is named Faith, and ventures into a dark forest. There the first person he meets is a mysterious "traveler" who carries a staff "which bore the likeness of a great black snake." Deep in the forest the young man discovers a group engaged in satanic worship, which ironically is comprised of those from his village whom he had believed to be most pious. Feeling a sudden "sympathy of all that was wicked in his heart," he is overcome with the temptation to join the "loathsome brotherhood." By the end of the story, he has entirely lost his Faith. The meanings of the allegorical emblems are clear and specific: the dark forest represents temptation, the traveler the devil, and the wife the religious piety that the initially "Good Man" abandons.

A symbol, in contrast, presents the image but leaves the subject that it represents open to a wide range of possible interpretations. A case in point is the poetry of William Blake, who was trained as an engraver and was by nature a visionary; his poems are full of complex **symbolism**. An example is his enigmatic lyric "The Sick Rose," in which the blighted flower might represent many forms of human suffering and corruption. Often, a longer work will contain a complex symbol that enlarges the LITERAL meaning of the story. Some signs of its **symbolic** importance might be its repeated appearances, especially at key points in the narrative, such as the climax or the conclusion; its close connection with the fate of the protagonist; and its detailed description.

In the course of Shakespeare's *Othello*, the handkerchief emerges as a symbolic object. The hero's first courtship gift to his bride, Desdemona, it is introduced at the midpoint of the tragedy, just after the villainous Iago has begun to convince Othello of the lie that Desdemona is having an affair with his junior officer, the handsome Cassio. Desdemona loses the handkerchief in the process of trying to cure a headache that Othello has developed. She offers to "bind [his head] hard," a folk remedy for a migraine. The ache comes supposedly from getting too little sleep, but in fact is in itself symbolic of

Othello's supposed cuckoldry. Popular legend in Shakespeare's day held that a wife's infidelity caused horns to grow on her betrayed husband's head, a painful process. Impatiently, Othello knocks the delicate cloth away with the words, "Your napkin [handkerchief] is too little." This line marks the climax of the play, the point at which Iago's poisonous influence has become too strong to be counteracted by Desdemona's love.

The neglected handkerchief is found by Iago's wife Emilia, Desdemona's lady in waiting, whom her husband has often urged to steal it. She gives it to Iago in a vain attempt to please him, and he then plants it in Cassio's bedchamber. Cassio admires the rich embroidery work and asks his mistress to sew a copy of it before the unknown owner can demand its return. Iago convinces the distraught husband that Cassio's possession of the handkerchief is evidence that Desdemona has given it to this new lover: it is the "ocular proof" of her infidelity that Othello has demanded. Only at the end of the play, after Othello has been driven to murder his beloved wife, does he discover the truth about the accessory that has so often changed hands, and meanings, in the course of the play. A symbol in a particular work, then, is often subtle and ambiguous, which makes for both its richness and the challenge of interpreting its possible meanings.

Atmosphere ◀

Atmosphere, a term taken from meteorology, means the predominant mood or TONE in all or part of a literary work. It may, for example, be joyous, tranquil, melancholy, eerie, tense, or ominous. The atmosphere, which may be suggested by such factors as the SETTING, DIALOGUE, DICTION, and SELECTION OF DETAILS in the narrative, usually foreshadows expectations about the outcome of the events. For example, Shakespeare's *Macbeth* begins with the following stage direction: *Thunder and lightning. Enter three WITCHES.* Immediately, the atmosphere becomes ominous as the storm in the natural world is linked with evil supernatural forces. The witches speak in curt TROCHAIC TETRAMETER COUPLETS, more a chant than naturalistic DIALOGUE. They also utter disturbing PARADOXES, such as "Fair is foul, and foul is fair," which suggest their satanic origins and deceptive purposes. The object of their talk adds to the ominous tone, for even before Macbeth has appeared, the witches are planning to "meet with" him "when the battle's lost and won."

The PARADOX signals the contradictory portrait of Macbeth that the play will develop: we soon discover that he is a brave and victorious soldier, whose daring exploits have won the military battle to which they ALLUDE. At the same time, he is secretly ambitious to gain the throne. By ruthlessly pursuing his ambition, he will lose the moral "battle." The Elizabethan audience would have been horrified at such an illegal succession to the throne. Therefore, the witches' intense focus on Macbeth foreshadows his corruption and the disruption to the natural order that it will create. Fittingly, at the end of the brief scene, the hags summon their satanic spirits, a cat and a toad, and prepare to "hover through the fog and filthy air" to the barren "heath" where they will confront Macbeth. The SETTING, DIALOGUE, DICTION, and descriptive DETAILS establish the tense, eerie atmosphere that will prevail throughout the tragedy.

An example of eerie, ominous atmosphere from narrative FICTION is "The Fall of the House of Usher" by Edgar Allan Poe, an acknowledged master of atmospheric effects. This is the SHORT STORY's opening:

> During the whole of a dull, dark, and soundless day in the autumn of the year, when the clouds hung oppressively low in the heavens, I had been passing alone, on horseback, through a singularly dreary tract of country; and at length found myself, as the shades of the evening drew on, within view of the melancholy House of Usher. I know not how it was—but, with the first glimpse of the building, a sense of insufferable gloom pervaded my spirit. I say insufferable; for the feeling was unrelieved by any of that half-pleasurable, because poetic, sentiment, with which the mind usually receives even the sternest natural images of the desolate or terrible. I looked upon the scene before me—upon the mere house, and the simple landscape features of the domain, upon the bleak walls, upon the vacant eye-like windows, upon a few rank sedges, and upon a few white trunks of decayed trees—with an utter depression of soul which I can compare to no earthly sensation more properly than to the after-dream of the reveler upon opium: the bitter lapse into everyday life, the hideous dropping off of the veil. There was an iciness, a sinking, a sickening of the heart, an unredeemed dreariness of thought which no goading of the imagination could torture into aught of the sublime.

Virtually every feature of the passage contributes to the atmosphere. The setting is a "dull, dark" autumn day in a desolate place that contains only a dilapidated mansion. The long, COMPLEX sentences are full of CONCRETE details, such as "white trunks of decayed trees" and "bleak walls." The oppressive tone is reinforced by FIGURATIVE descriptions—the SIMILE of the "vacant eye-like windows" and the METAPHORICAL comparison of the "utter depression" that the scene evokes to the "bitter lapse into everyday life" of the after-effects of an opium dream. The FIRST-PERSON NARRATOR does not allow such visual IMAGERY to stand alone, however. He states outright the effects of arriving at the scene on horseback: the "sense of insufferable gloom" and "sickening of the heart" that "so unnerved [him] in the contemplation of the House of Usher." This statement adds undertones of threat and revulsion to the atmosphere of gloom and desolation.

EXERCISES: Imagery, Symbolism, and Atmosphere

I. For each of the following passages:
- Describe the physical senses—sight, hearing, smell, touch, temperature, or movement—that the IMAGERY involves or evokes.
- Identify not only LITERAL objects, actions, and scenes but also VEHICLES of METAPHORS and SIMILES that contribute to the IMAGERY.
- Explain the effects of the IMAGERY on the tone and meaning of the passage.

1. They eat beans mostly, this old yellow pair.
   Dinner is a casual affair.
   Plain chipware on a plain and creaking wood.
   Tin flatware.

   Two who are Mostly Good.   5
   Two who have lived their day,
   But keep on putting on their clothes
   And putting things away.

   And remembering . . .
   Remembering, with twinklings and twinges,   10
   As they lean over the beans in their rented back room that is full of
      beads and receipts and dolls and clothes, tobacco crumbs, vases
      and fringes.   —GWENDOLYN BROOKS, "The Bean Eaters"

2. I have lived long enough. My way of life
   Is fall'n into the sere,[1] the yellow leaf,
   And that which should accompany old age,

---

1. Withered.

That the fixed sentinels almost receive
The secret whispers of each others' watch.
Fire answers fire, and through their paly[5] flames
Each battle sees the other's umbered[6] face.
Steed threatens steed, in high and boastful neighs   10
Piercing the night's dull ear, and from the tents
The armourers, accomplishing[7] the knights,
With busy hammers closing rivets up,
Give dreadful note of preparation.

Repetition

Intentional—as opposed to careless or unintentional—**repetition** of sounds, words, phrasing, or concepts is used in literary works to create unity and emphasis. The effects of repetition on the work's TONE and meaning vary with the context and with the form of the repeated element. Special forms of the repetition of sound in POETRY include RHYME, METER, and such SOUND PATTERNS as ALLITERATION and ASSONANCE. The repetition of complete words or phrases occurs in ANAPHORA and the REFRAIN. In POETRY and FICTION, as well as in DRAMA, patterns of the repetition of words or phrases are important to many forms of SYMBOLISM and IMAGERY.

In a less specialized sense, repetition of words can signal a speaker's thoughts and emotions. For example, at the end of Shakespeare's *King Lear*, the old king is attempting to comprehend the horrifying reality that his best-loved daughter is dead, and that he has been indirectly responsible for her loss. Addressing her lifeless body, he emphasizes his devastating realization that she will "come no more" in a BLANK VERSE line that consists of a single repeated word: "Never, never, never, never, never!" The repetition expresses Lear's shock, as well as his heartbreak.

Some authors use a repeated word or phrase as a means of CHARACTERIZATION, especially in depicting FLAT, as opposed to THREE-DIMENSIONAL, CHARACTERS. That is a favorite device of the Victorian novelist Charles Dickens. For example, the devious Uriah Heep in Dickens's *David Copperfield* (1850) always describes himself as "umble"—the cockney pronunciation of "humble"—even as he schemes with ruthless ambition to take over the business of his gullible employer and to force Mr. Wickfield's innocent daughter Agnes

---

5. Pale.
6. Shadowed. "Battle": army.
7. Equipping.

▼

into a loveless marriage. In addition, Dickens often gives a character a favorite tag line that sums up his or her outlook or values. For example, each of the Micawbers, the kindly but hopelessly impractical couple who provide the young David with shabby room and board, has a favorite catch phrase. Mr. Micawber's is the conviction that "something will turn up" to rescue him and his growing family from debtors' prison, and Mrs. Micawber's is the melodramatic assertion, "I never will desert Mr. Micawber," even as she pawns their few possessions and begs petty loans to keep the Micawber household intact a while longer.

Selection and Order of Details ◀

The **selection** and the **order of the details** in a literary work are crucial to its meaning and TONE. Because the form of a POEM, a PLAY, or a work of FICTION may look so inevitable and move so smoothly on the page, it is easy to forget that the work is based on a series of deliberate choices that the author makes in the course of writing and revising it. Such choices include both the nature and relative specificity of the details and the order in which they appear. For example, John Cheever's SHORT STORY "Reunion" opens with the following paragraph:

> The last time I saw my father was in Grand Central Station. I was going from my grandmother's in the Adirondacks to a cottage on the Cape that my mother had rented, and I wrote my father that I would be in New York between trains for an hour and a half, and asked if we could have lunch together. His secretary wrote to say that he would meet me at the information booth at noon, and at twelve o'clock sharp I saw him coming through the crowd. He was a stranger to me—my mother divorced him three years ago and I hadn't seen him since—but as soon as I saw him I felt that he was my father, my flesh and blood, my future and my doom. I knew that when I was grown I would be something like him; I would have to plan my campaigns within his limitations. He was a big, good-looking man, and I was terribly happy to see him again. He struck me on the back and shook my hand. "Hi, Charlie," he said. "Hi, boy. I'd like to take you up to my club, but it's in the Sixties, and if you have to catch an early train I guess we'd better get something to eat around here." He put his arm around me, and I smelled my father the way my mother sniffs a rose. It was a rich compound of whiskey, after-shave lotion, shoe polish, woolens, and the rankness of a mature male. I hoped that

▼

someone would see us together. I wished that we could be photo-
graphed. I wanted some record of our having been together.

The details imply that the FIRST-PERSON NARRATOR is a teenage boy:
his points of reference are the parent-figures in his life, but he is old
enough to travel alone and to initiate the contact with his father by
writing a letter. The main impressions that the details create—the
boy's pride in the moment and longing for male company—are conveyed by his eager response to the sight, movement, and smell of
his long-absent father. He is proud of the man's good looks, and he
instantly recognizes their bond: the heritage of "flesh and blood"
and the sense that his father's appearance and character represent his
own "future" and "doom."

The father's first actions are aggressively friendly: he claps the
boy on the back, shakes his hand, offers to buy him lunch, and
"put[s] his arm around" him. That close contact evokes Charlie's
humorous SIMILE comparing his relish of his father's admittedly "rank"
blend of smells to his mother's pleasure in "sniff[ing] a rose." The
humor implies his realization that his reaction is excessive. At the
same time, his wish, REPEATED three times, that he could have some
means to preserve the moment suggests the loneliness of the father-
less boy and his fervent need for the relationship to be sustained.

Other details, however, qualify the largely joyous TONE of the
passage and provide ominous foreshadowing. It is not the father but
"his secretary" who responds to the boy's letter, and then only with
factual information about the time and place of the meeting, as if
she were making a business appointment. The wording of the sentence about the parents' divorce shows that the mother initiated the
action, and that Charlie has had no contact with his father in the
intervening three years. That last fact is the more surprising, given
the man's extroverted nature and his seeming eagerness to claim
Charlie as his "boy" at their moment of meeting.

Another troubling factor is the order in which the NARRATOR lists
the various scents emanating from his father: the first is that of "whis-
key." That detail seems especially ominous given the time of day—
noon, which means that the drinking must have taken place in the
morning—and the nature of the occasion—the first reunion of father
and son after a three-year gap. Such selection and order of details foreshadow the disillusioning course that the encounter will take. As the
first sentence of the story states, this will be "the last time" that Charlie
sees his father. The meaning of the phrase is not its factual sense, "the
previous time," but the final occasion on which son and father meet.

See also: CONCRETE DICTION, IMAGERY, SYMBOLISM, and DIALOGUE.

▼

EXERCISES: Repetition and Selection and Order of Details

I. For each of the following passages:
- Identify any REPETITION and/or describe the SELECTION AND ORDER OF DETAILS.
- Explain the effects of those techniques on the TONE and the meaning of the passage.

1. *The following description is of the outcome of Dr. Victor Frankenstein's attempt to create human life in his laboratory:*

> It was a dreary night of November that I beheld the accomplishment of my toils. With an anxiety that almost amounted to agony, I collected the instruments of life around me, that I might infuse a spark of being into the lifeless thing that lay at my feet. It was already one in the morning; the rain pattered dismally against the panes, and my candle was nearly burnt out, when, by the glimmer of the half-extinguished light, I saw the dull yellow eye of the creature open; it breathed hard, and a convulsive motion agitated its limbs.
>
> How can I describe my emotions at this catastrophe, or how delineate the wretch whom with such infinite pains and care I had endeavoured to form? His limbs were in proportion, and I had selected his features as beautiful. Beautiful! Great God! His yellow skin scarcely covered the work of muscles and arteries beneath; his hair was of a lustrous black, and flowing; his teeth of a pearly whiteness; but these luxuriances only formed a more horrid contrast with his watery eyes, that seemed almost of the same colour as the dun-white sockets in which they were set, his shriveled complexion and straight black lips. —MARY SHELLEY, *Frankenstein*

2. Still[1] to be neat, still to be dressed,
As you were going to a feast;
Still to be powdered, still perfumed;
Lady, it is to be presumed,
Though art's hid causes are not found,   5
All is not sweet, all is not sound.

   Give me a look, give me a face
That makes simplicity a grace;
Robes loosely flowing, hair as free;
Such sweet neglect more taketh me   10
Than all the adulteries of art.
They strike mine eyes, but not my heart.
                                        —BEN JONSON, "Still to Be Neat"

---

1. Always.

▼

3. *The following passage, set in the 1920s, describes the visit of a "deputa-*
    tion" of political leaders in a Mississippi town who have gone to confront
    an elderly citizen about her failure to pay taxes:

> [They] knocked at the door through which no visitor had
> passed since she ceased giving china-painting lessons eight or ten
> years earlier. They were admitted by the old Negro[2] into a dim hall
> from which a stairway mounted into still more shadow. It smelled
> of dust and disuse—a close, dank smell. The Negro led them into
> the parlor. It was furnished with heavy, leather-covered furniture.
> When the Negro opened the blinds of one window, they could see
> that the leather was cracked; and when they sat down, a faint dust
> rose sluggishly about their thighs, spinning with slow motes in the
> single sun-ray. On a tarnished gilt easel before the fireplace stood a
> crayon portrait of Miss Emily's father.[3]
>
> They rose when she entered—a small, fat woman in black,
> with a thin gold chain descending to her waist and vanishing into
> her belt, leaning on an ebony cane with a tarnished gold head. Her
> skeleton was small and spare; perhaps that was why what would
> have been merely plumpness in another was obesity in her. She
> looked bloated, like a body submerged in motionless water, and of
> that pallid hue. Her eyes, lost in the fatty ridges of her face, looked
> like two small pieces of coal pressed into a lump of dough as they
> moved from one face to another while the visitors stated their
> errand.   —WILLIAM FAULKNER, "A Rose for Emily"

4. *This is the conclusion to a description of an "oil-soaked" gas station that*
    begins with the line: "Oh, but it is dirty!"

> Some comic books provide
> the only note of color—
> of certain color. They lie
> upon a big dim doily
> draping a taboret[4]   5
> (part of the set), beside
> a big hirsute begonia.
>
> Why the extraneous plant?
> Why the taboret?
> Why, oh why, the doily?   10

---

2. Her servant.
3. Now dead.
4. A drum-shaped table.

▼

(Embroidered in daisy stitch
with marguerites,[5] I think,
and heavy with gray crochet.)

Somebody embroidered the doily.
Somebody waters the plant,   15
or oils it, maybe. Somebody
arranges the rows of cans
so that they softly say:
ESSO—SO—SO—SO[6]
To high-strung automobiles.   20
Somebody loves us all.

–Elizabeth Bishop, "Filling Station"

II. Analysis of a long passage

The following passage from Jack London's "To Build a Fire" occurs after the PROTAGONIST, a prospector in the Klondike, has fallen through the ice of a stream and wet his feet. With the temperature at seventy-five below zero, he realizes that his one chance of survival is to build a fire that will let him dry his moccasins and prevent his feet from freezing. He has taken off his mittens to light a match, but that exposure causes his fingers to freeze. As the passage opens, he is beating his hands against his sides to try to revive the feeling in his fingers. Explain how the SELECTION and ORDER OF DETAILS and the REPETITION of words and ideas reveal the narrator's TONE and suggest the emotional impact of the event that he describes.

After a while he was aware of the first faraway signals of sensation in his beaten fingers. The faint tingling grew stronger till it evolved into a stinging ache that was excruciating, but which the man hailed with satisfaction. He stripped the mitten from his right hand and fetched forth the birchbark. The exposed fingers were quickly going numb again. Next he brought out his bunch of sulphur matches. But the tremendous cold had already driven the life out of his fingers. In his effort to separate one match from the others, the whole bunch fell in the snow. He tried to pick it up out of the snow, but failed. The dead fingers could neither touch nor clutch. He was very careful. He drove the thought of his freezing feet, and nose, and cheeks, out of his mind, devoting his whole soul to the matches. He watched, using the sense of vision in place of that of touch, and when he saw his fingers on each side of the

---

5. Small daisies.
6. Brand name, later changed to "Exxon."

bunch, he closed them—that is, he willed to close them, for the wires were down, and the fingers did not obey. He pulled the mitten on the right hand, and beat it fiercely against his knee. Then with both mittened hands, he scooped the bunch of matches, along with much snow, into his lap. Yet he was no better off.

After some manipulation, he managed to get the bunch between his mittened hands. In this fashion he carried it to his mouth. The ice crackled and snapped when by a violent effort he opened his mouth. He drew the lower jaw in, curled the upper lip out of the way, and scraped the bunch with his upper teeth in order to separate a match. He succeeded in getting one, which he dropped on his lap. He was no better off. He could not pick it up. Then he devised a way. He picked it up in his teeth and scratched it on his leg. Twenty times he scratched before he succeeded in lighting it. As it flamed he held it with his teeth to the birchbark. But the burning brimstone went up his nostrils and into his lungs, causing him to cough spasmodically. The match fell into the snow and went out.

Narration

Narration refers to the act of telling a story, whether in prose or in verse, and also to the means of telling it. The main **narrative** forms in prose are the NOVEL, the NOVELLA, and the SHORT STORY. Narrative forms in verse are the EPIC, and other poems that contain a PLOT and individualized CHARACTERS. The DRAMA is also narrative in the sense that it tells a story, but it does so directly, with characters who act out the plot on a stage and who speak for themselves. In its broad sense, narration means all of the aspects of a story and all of the techniques available to the author:

- the nature of the NARRATOR
- the choice of POINT OF VIEW
- the ROLES that the characters play in the PLOT
- the SETTING in which the story takes place
- the means of conveying the CHARACTERIZATION
- the use of DIALOGUE
- the STRUCTURE
- the THEMES that emerge, and
- the TONE that the work conveys.

Standing behind the fictional NARRATIVE is the authorial VOICE implied by these various choices.

Voice

The **narrator** of a literary work, of FICTION or POETRY, is the one who tells the story. His or her identity differs from that of the author, because the narrator is always in some sense the author's invention. The narrator often differs from the author in age, gender, outlook, or circumstances. For example, Mark Twain's NOVEL *Adventures of Huckleberry Finn* is narrated by a naïve teenage boy; Langston Hughes's DRAMATIC MONOLOGUE "Mother to Son" by a poor, aging woman; and Edgar Allan Poe's SHORT STORY "The Cask of Amontillado" by an insane murderer. In such works, it is easy not to confuse the narrator with the author.

In some works, though, the reader may have to guard against the temptation to equate the writer with his or her invented speaker. This is true in the cases of Edith Wharton's sympathetic newcomer in the NOVELLA *Ethan Frome*, F. Scott Fitzgerald's earnest moralist Nick Carraway in the NOVEL *The Great Gatsby*, and the several narrators of Shakespeare's sonnets.

The key point is that the voice of the author shapes the fictional narrative; the narrator is simply an element of the story. The author's voice is implied by the convictions and values by which characters and events are judged. In turn, the way that the story is told evokes responses and judgments from the reader.

POINT OF VIEW

Point of view can be identified by the pronoun that the NARRATOR uses to tell the story. "I" (or, occasionally, "we" for the plural form) for the FIRST-PERSON; "he," "she," or "they" for the THIRD-PERSON; and "you" for the rarely used SECOND-PERSON.

First-Person

The **first-person** POINT OF VIEW has the advantages of immediacy and directness. It invites the reader to listen to a speaker who seems to be relating first-hand experience. In the following passage, Huck Finn, who has been living the hard but free life of a homeless orphan, describes the trials of undergoing the kindly widow Douglas's attempts to "sivilize" him:

> The widow she cried over me, and called me a poor lost lamb, and she called me a lot of other names, too, but she never meant no harm by it. She put me in them new clothes again, and I couldn't do nothing but sweat and sweat, and feel all cramped up. Well, then the old thing commenced again. The widow rung a bell for supper, and you had to come to time. When you got to the table you couldn't go right to eating, but you had to wait for the widow to tuck down her head and grumble a little over the victuals, though there warn't really anything the matter with them. That is, nothing only everything was cooked by itself. In a barrel of odds and ends it is different; things get mixed up, and the juice kind of swaps around, and the things go better.

The narration sounds fresh and authentic. That effect comes from the humorous first-person voice, with its homely language. Huck evokes sympathy through his restlessness at having to follow rules and learn manners, and humor by his mistaking of the widow's saying of grace at the table for "grumbl[ing]."

The first person also imposes limitations on the teller, however. The NARRATOR can relate only what he or she might have witnessed, and then only with the degree of understanding appropriate to his or her circumstances and character. For example, a first-person narrator who is a child, such as Huck Finn, or whose mind is afflicted, such as Poe's mad speaker, cannot convincingly present a situation with the depth or subtlety of a more sophisticated or better balanced speaker. Nor can a first-person narrator logically describe his or her own death. Such works as Emily Dickinson's "I heard a Fly buzz—when I died" and William Faulkner's *As I Lay Dying*, however, create enormous shock value by defying that logical impossibility. See also: UNRELIABLE NARRATOR, STRUCTURAL IRONY.

Third-Person

The **third-person** point of view presents a NARRATOR that has a much broader and, usually, objective view of characters and events. Third-person narration falls into two major subtypes. An **omniscient third-person** narrator can enter the mind of any character, evaluate motives and explain feelings, and recount the background and predict the outcome of situations. The other major type of third-person point of view is called the **third-person limited**, which means that the narrator describes events only from the perspective of one, or sometimes, a select few characters.

One example of a work narrated in the omniscient third-person is George Eliot's *Middlemarch* (1872), a study of "provincial life" in Victorian England. The novel takes us into the thoughts and motives of a wide variety of characters during courtship and marriage and covers such broad social issues as political activism, religion, women's rights, and the development of medical science. Other examples are Stephen Crane's short story "The Open Boat" (1897–98), which follows the fortunes of four shipwrecked men in a small lifeboat as they try to reach land safely; and E. M. Forster's *A Passage to India* (1924), which recounts the complex tensions and bonds among various English officials and tourists and the native Indian population during the British Raj. The advantages of the omniscient point of view are the wisdom and authority that it suggests and the unlimited range of material that it can cover. It can, though, create a feeling of distance, and so reduce the degree of connection between readers and characters.

An omniscient narrator who offers philosophical or moral commentary on the story's characters and events is called an **intrusive narrator**. That technique was especially popular in nineteenth-century fiction, in such novels as William Makepeace Thackeray's *Vanity Fair* (1848). The account is punctuated by sly, often ironic judgments on the motives and actions of the characters as well as on the society. For example, after quoting a long, flattering speech to a wealthy heiress by a man eager to gain her friendship for himself and his daughters, the narrator of *Vanity Fair* interrupts the story to comment:

> There is little doubt that old Osborne believed all he said, and that the girls were quite earnest in their protestations of affection for Miss Swartz. People in Vanity Fair fasten on to rich folks quite naturally. If the simplest people are disposed to look not a little kindly on great Prosperity, (for I defy any member of the British public to say that the notion of Wealth has not something awful and pleasing to him; and you, if you are told that the man next to you at dinner has got half a million, not to look at him with a certain interest;)—if the simple look benevolently on money, how much more do your old worldlings regard it! Their affections rush out to meet and welcome money.

The narrator's IRONY is signaled by his exposure of the real motive for Osborne's sudden "affection" in Miss Swartz's "Wealth," capitalized along with "Prosperity" for extra emphasis. Also, he extends the target of his satire to involve not only the "people in Vanity Fair," the stereotype of society that he is depicting, but "any member of the British public." That includes, in a sudden shift to the SECOND-PERSON POINT OF VIEW, the reader at an imaginary dinner party.

A third-person narrator whose presence is **merely implied** is called an **objective narrator**. That technique, more favored in recent times, is subtler. It is used in such works as Bernard Malamud's *The Assistant* (1957), a novel about a lonely young drifter who is inspired by his relationship with a warm Jewish family to change his religion and way of life, and in several of Ernest Hemingway's short stories. In Hemingway's "The End of Something," the protagonist, Nick Adams, has just admitted to his girlfriend that he no longer loves her. They have been fishing, and she responds only that she is going to take the rowboat back while he walks. He offers to push it off for her, and the story ends with the following section:

"You don't need to," she said. She was afloat in the boat on the water with the moonlight on it. Nick went back and lay down with his face in the blanket by the fire. He could hear Marjorie rowing on the water.

He lay there for a long time. He lay there while he heard Bill come into the clearing, walking around the woods. He felt Bill come up to the fire. Bill didn't touch him, either.

"Did she go all right?" Bill said.

"Oh, yes," Nick said, lying, his face in the blanket.

"Have a scene?"

"No, there wasn't any scene."

"How do you feel?"

"Oh, go away, Bill! Go away for a while." Bill selected a sandwich from the lunch basket and walked over to have a look at the rods.

We are left to infer the characters' emotions from the spare, matter-of-fact report of their DIALOGUE and their actions. Nick is feeling depressed and guilty over the breakup. That is signaled by his position, his face hidden in the blanket, and by his curt replies. Marjorie is hurt and determined not to react. Bill's words suggest his well-meaning yet prying curiosity, which provokes Nick's irritation.

The **third-person limited**, as stated above, restricts the point of view to the understanding and experience of one or, in some cases, of a few characters. A poignant example is James Joyce's "A Painful Case." It focuses on the perspective of a bitter intellectual who discovers too late that he has rejected the one person who has ever loved him. In the following scene, the protagonist, Mr. Duffy, is reacting to a newspaper account of the woman's death. It reveals that in the four years since he ended their relationship, she has continued to be neglected by her husband and grown daughter, taken to drink, and died by walking in front of a train:

> As he sat there, living over his life with her and evoking alternately the two images in which he now conceived her, he realized that she was dead, that she had ceased to exist, that she had become a memory. He began to feel ill at ease. He asked himself what else could he have done. He could not have lived with her openly. He had done what seemed to him best. How was he to blame? Now that she was gone he understood how lonely her life must have been, sitting night after night alone in that room. His life would be lonely too until he, too, died, ceased to exist, became a memory—if anyone remembered him.

▼

The limited perspective follows Duffy's changing feelings. He goes from growing discomfort with his former self-righteousness to a first realization of his own guilt to sudden empathy for the woman's situation. Finally, he arrives at the realization that he has doomed himself to share her terrible loneliness. An example of the third-person limited point of view used to represent the perspective of a series of characters is Henry James's *The Wings of the Dove*. That point of view takes us into the minds of the three members of a love triangle: a beautiful, socially ambitious young woman determined to marry well; the sensitive, penniless young man who loves her and with whom she is in love; and the generous, mortally ill young heiress whom they pretend to befriend and who also falls in love with the man.

The third-person limited has the advantages of both the immediacy of the first person and the authority and range of the third-person omniscient. Perhaps for those reasons, it is the most frequently used point of view in all three of the fictional genres— the NOVEL, the SHORT STORY, and the NOVELLA.

▶ ## Second-Person

The third major point of view is the **second-person**, in which the narrator addresses the audience directly using the pronoun "you" and assumes that the audience is experiencing the events along with the narrator. That implied audience may be the reader, a character who appears later in the story, or a listener who is never identified, such as a therapist in whom the narrator is confiding. The second-person occurs most frequently as a temporary departure from one of the other points of view. For example, Holden Caufield, the troubled teenage FIRST-PERSON NARRATOR in J. D. Salinger's *The Catcher in the Rye* (1951), introduces the younger sister he adores. Then he says several times with uncharacteristic enthusiasm, "You'd like her. . . . I swear to God you'd like her." Holden may be speaking to a sympathetic reader or to one of the doctors at the "crumby place" where, he tells us on the first page, he has been sent to recover from "some madman stuff" he has suffered. In either case, the shift in both his perspective and his attitude is striking.

John Cheever's "The Swimmer" (1964) is a THIRD-PERSON LIM-ITED story about an apparently carefree suburbanite who decides to return home after an afternoon poolside party by swimming across the pools owned by his neighbors. One of the first hints of the devastating truth about his situation comes in a sudden switch to the second-person point of view as he waits to cross a busy, littered highway:

> Had you gone for a Sunday afternoon ride that day you might have seen him, close to naked, standing on the shoulders of Route 424, waiting for a chance to cross. You might have wondered if he was the victim of foul play, had his car broken down, or was he merely a fool.

His vulnerability and isolation foreshadow the terrible emptiness that awaits him at his journey's end.

The second-person has also been used effectively in entire works. One example is Jay McInerney's *Bright Lights, Big City* (1984), which follows the nameless PROTAGONIST in his frantic attempts to immerse himself in the night life of New York City in order to escape the chaos into which his life is falling. By the end, he is barely functional but more humble and self-aware:

> You get down on your knees and tear open the bag. The smell of warm dough envelops you. The first bite sticks in your throat and you almost gag. You will have to go slowly. You will have to learn everything all over again.

Not surprisingly, the use of the second-person point of view is relatively rare. While it has the immediacy of the FIRST-PERSON, it can have the off-putting effects of seeming highly self-conscious and of calling constant attention to the process of narration. It also limits the kinds of scenes that can effectively be related through such constant back-and-forth involvement between narrator and audience.

EXERCISE: Point of View

For each of the following passages:

- Identify the POINT OF VIEW: FIRST-PERSON, SECOND-PERSON, THIRD-PERSON LIMITED, or THIRD-PERSON OMNISCIENT.
- If the POINT OF VIEW is THIRD-PERSON OMNISCIENT, state whether the NARRATOR is INTRUSIVE or OBJECTIVE.
- Explain why the term or terms apply.
- Describe the effects of the POINT OF VIEW on the meaning and the TONE of the passage.

1. In walks these three girls in nothing but bathing suits. I'm in the third checkout slot, with my back to the door, so I don't see them

▼

until they're over by the bread. The one that caught my eye first was the one in the plaid green two-piece. She was a chunky kid, with a good tan and a sweet broad soft-looking can with those two crescents of white just under it, where the sun never seems to hit, at the top of the backs of her legs. I stood there with my hand on a box of HiHo crackers trying to remember if I rang it up or not.

—JOHN UPDIKE, "A & P"

2. [Miss Bates] enjoyed a most uncommon degree of popularity for a woman neither young, handsome, rich, nor married. [She] stood in the very worst predicament in the world for having much of the public favour; and she had no intellectual superiority to make atonement to herself, or frighten those who might hate her into outward respect. She had never boasted either beauty or cleverness. Her youth had passed without distinction, and her middle of life was devoted to the care of a failing mother, and the endeavour to make a small income go as far as possible. And yet she was a happy woman, and a woman whom no one named without goodwill. It was her own universal good-will and contented temper which worked such wonders. She loved every body, was interested in every body's happiness, quick-sighted to every body's merits; thought herself a most fortunate creature, and surrounded with blessings. . . .

—JANE AUSTEN, *Emma*

3. *This stanza follows a description of soldiers caught in a poison gas attack during World War I:*

If in some smothering dreams you too could pace
Behind the wagon that we flung him in,
And watch the white eyes writhing in his face,
His hanging face, like a devil's sick of sin;
If you could hear, at every jolt, the blood   5
Come gargling from the froth-corrupted lungs,
Obscene as cancer, bitter as the cud
Of vile, incurable sores on innocent tongues—
My friend, you would not tell with such high zest
To children ardent for some desperate glory,   10
The old Lie: Dulce et decorum est
Pro patria mori.[1]   —WILFRED OWEN, "Dulce Et Decorum Est"

4. The morning of June 27th was clear and sunny, with the fresh warmth of a full-summer day; the flowers were blossoming pro-

---

1. Horace, *Ode* 3.2.13: "It is sweet and decorous to die for one's country."

fusely and the grass was richly green. The people of the village began to gather in the square, between the post office and the bank, around ten o'clock; in some towns there were so many people that the lottery took two days and had to be started on June 26th, but in this village, where there were only about three hundred people, the whole lottery took less than two hours, so it could begin at ten o'clock in the morning and still be through in time to allow the villagers to get home for noon dinner.

—SHIRLEY JACKSON, "The Lottery"

5. I had a test today. I think I faled it. and I think that maybe now they wont use me. What happind is a nice young man was in the room and he had some white cards with ink spilled all over them. He sed Charlie what do you see on this card. I was very skared even tho I had my rabits foot in my pockit because when I was a kid I always faled tests in school and I spilled ink to.

    I told him I saw a inkblot. He said yes and it made me feel good. I thot that was all but when I got up to go he stopped me. He said now sit down Charlie we are not thru yet.

    —DANIEL KEYES, "Flowers for Algernon"

6. Now the broad road was crossed. The lane began, smoky and dark. Women in shawls and men's tweed caps hurried by. Men hung over the palings; the children played in the doorways. A low hum came from the mean little cottages. In some of them there was a flicker of light, and a shadow, crab-like, moved across the window. Laura bent her head and hurried on. She wished now that she had put on a coat. How her frock shone! And the big hat with the velvet streamer—if only it was another hat! Were the people looking at her? They must be. It was a mistake to have come; she knew all along it was a mistake. Should she go back even now?

    —KATHERINE MANSFIELD, "The Garden-Party"

CHARACTERIZATION

Characterization means the techniques by which an author of a work of FICTION, DRAMA, or NARRATIVE POETRY represents the moral, intellectual, and emotional natures of the characters. In *Aspects of the Novel* (1927), the critic and novelist E. M. Forster introduced the terms FLAT and ROUND CHARACTERS to describe the extent to which literary characters are developed. In analyzing the methods by which authors depict characters, a useful distinction is between SHOWING and TELLING.

▼

► Flat Characters vs. Round Characters

A **flat character**, also called a **two-dimensional character**, is more a type than an individual, and stays essentially the same throughout the work. In Charles Dickens's *Great Expectations*, for example, the good-hearted Joe Gargery and the embittered, man-hating Miss Havisham are flat characters. The term "two-dimensional" refers to a line such as is used in drawing a sketch. It should not be mistakenly called "one-dimensional," which means a single point and therefore does not apply. A **round**, or **three-dimensional**, **character**, in contrast, is multifaceted and subject to change and growth. He or she is also capable of inconsistencies, and in those ways similar to an actual human being. Pip, the PROTAGONIST/NARRATOR of Dickens's novel, for example, changes enormously from the naïve, sweet-tempered child of the early chapters as he grows to manhood, discovers new sides of his nature, and confronts various crises.

Some characters may surprise readers with their three-dimensionality as a work goes on. In Shakespeare's *Othello*, Emilia, the oppressed wife of Iago, seems at first to be a simple and largely silent TYPE rather than a round character. As she comes to realize the extent of her husband's villainy, however, she finds her voice and emerges as clear-sighted, insightful, and courageous. The reader must encounter round characters in several different contexts in order to gauge their complexities and inconsistencies. Flat characters, in contrast, tend to reveal their essence from the outset and to change little.

This is not to imply that characters must be round to be effective. Their relative level of development depends on their role in the action and on the style of the work in which they appear. Usually, except in long, complex novels such as Tolstoy's *Anna Karenina* and Eliot's *Middlemarch*, there is space for only a few ROUND characters, and sometimes for the PROTAGONIST alone to be shown THREE-DIMENSIONALLY. Also, characters in an adventure story, such as *The Lord of the Rings*; a SATIRE such as Jonathan Swift's *Gulliver's Travels*; or a farce, such as Shakespeare's *The Comedy of Errors*, remain FLAT in order to keep the reader's attention on more essential aspects of the work, such as PLOT and TONE.

Showing vs. Telling ◀

In depicting characters, authors use methods of either **showing** or **telling**. **Showing** means simply presenting characters' words and actions without commentary and so implying their motives, feelings, and values. That direct approach has been favored since the late nineteenth century. Masters of the technique have included Henry James, Anton Chekhov, Ernest Hemingway, and Nadine Gordimer.

Telling, in contrast, is the method by which the author describes, and comments on, characters' motives and values and often also passes judgment on characters and events, as a means of shaping the audience's response. That approach has been used by most of the great nineteenth-century novelists, for example, Jane Austen, George Eliot, Charles Dickens, and Leo Tolstoy, as well as by many of their modern successors, including E. M. Forster, Willa Cather, and D. H. Lawrence.

For a description of techniques that are crucial to characterizing the personages in a NOVEL, SHORT STORY, or DRAMA, see NARRATOR, POINT OF VIEW, and DIALOGUE.

EXERCISES: Characterization

I. Name a FLAT CHARACTER and a ROUND CHARACTER from two narratives—NOVELS, SHORT STORIES, or DRAMAS—that you have studied recently, and explain why that term applies.

II. Turn to the exercises on POINT OF VIEW and on DIALOGUE, and choose one passage that uses SHOWING to depict the characters and one that uses TELLING. Then explain why each of those terms applies.

ROLES IN THE PLOT

Most literary works of FICTION, DRAMA, and NARRATIVE POETRY contain a **plot**, a sequence of events leading to some sort of resolution. That resolution is designed to reveal the feelings, motives, and values of the characters. The main roles that the characters assume fall into three types: the PROTAGONIST, the ANTAGONIST, and the FOIL.

Protagonist

The **protagonist** (proh-TAG-ahn-ihst) is the main character in a work of DRAMA, FICTION, or NARRATIVE POETRY. The events of the work center on him or her, as does the reader's interest. Some examples are Elizabeth Bennet in Jane Austen's *Pride and Prejudice*, Macbeth in the Shakespearean tragedy of the same name, and Odysseus in Homer's epic *The Odyssey*. An alternative term for the protagonist is the **hero** or **heroine**. That term, however, has a connotation of nobility, dignity, and elevated status. While it is fitting for the chief character in an epic or a classic tragedy, it does not suit the petty flaws and lowly status of more ordinary protagonists, such as Holden Caulfield, the confused adolescent in J. D. Salinger's *The Catcher in the Rye*, or the downtrodden Willy Loman in Arthur Miller's *Death of a Salesman*. In other words, the broader term "protagonist" is preferable in most cases. Some complex works lack a single protagonist and instead shift the focus as different characters play a central role in various subplots and SETTINGS, as in Shakespeare's *Antony and Cleopatra* and E. M. Forster's *A Passage to India*.

Antagonist

In many works, the main character has an **antagonist** (an-TAG-ahn-ihst), a character that opposes the PROTAGONIST's goals and interests and so creates the major conflict in the work. Examples are Poseidon in Homer's *Odyssey*, the Olympian god of the sea who continually blocks Odysseus's attempts to reach his homeland, and Augustus Caesar in *Antony and Cleopatra*, who opposes Marc Antony's political ambitions as well as his passion for Cleopatra. If the antagonist has evil intentions, like Iago in *Othello*, he is called the **villain**. In some works, however, the protagonist is himself evil, like Shakespeare's Macbeth. In such cases, the antagonist—in *Macbeth*, Macduff serves that function—is portrayed as a sympathetic character.

In a broad sense, an antagonist need not be another character. It may be some larger force that challenges the protagonist, such as fate. In Sophocles's *Oedipus Rex*, fate defeats all of Oedipus's attempts to circumvent the dire prophecy made at his birth. In Jack London's "To Build a Fire," the antagonist is the paralyzing cold of the Klondike, while in Stephen Crane's *The Red Badge of Courage*, it is the traumatic effect of battle. The antagonist may also be internal, in the form of conflicting desires or values within the protagonist. In Charlotte Brontë's *Jane Eyre*, for example, the protagonist is torn between remaining with the man she loves in an adulterous relationship, or else obeying her conscience by leaving him for a life of emptiness and poverty.

A work may contain more than one sort of antagonist. Shakespeare's Hamlet, for example, has a human antagonist in his uncle Claudius, who has murdered Hamlet's father, seduced his mother, and seized the Danish throne. Hamlet, however, is also beset by the demands of fate, which has designated him the "scourge and minister" who must restore order to Denmark, even at the cost of his life. The third antagonist that Hamlet faces is internal, the conflict between his desire to take swift and violent action and a tendency to mull over choices and moral issues that keeps him from acting.

Foil ◄

A third kind of role that occurs in many works is that of the foil. He or she is a character who contrasts with the PROTAGONIST in ways that bring out moral, emotional, or intellectual qualities. Hamlet calls attention to that function just before his fatal duel with Laertes, the impulsive man of action who is his main foil in the play. The men are about to engage in what Hamlet believes is not a serious duel but a friendly demonstration of their skill with "foils," that is, swords. He has quarreled with Laertes earlier, and to make amends, he gives a flattering speech:

> I'll be your foil, Laertes. In mine ignorance
> Your skill shall, like a star i'th' darkest night,
> Stick fiery off indeed.

Here the PUN—"foil" in Shakespeare's day meant not only a rapier but a piece of thin metal foil on which jewels were placed to show off their sparkle—suggests both aspects of Laertes' relationship to the HERO. His roles are to oppose him in the conflict with Claudius, with whom Laertes is secretly allied, and to highlight Hamlet's honorable conduct and contemplative nature.

In Shakespeare's *Romeo and Juliet*, the hero has several foils: the cynical Mercutio, who mocks the romantic love that Romeo celebrates with Juliet; the hot-tempered Tybalt, who is obsessed with defending his family name in the feud that Romeo sees as senseless; and the sweet-tempered Benvolio, who strives only to be a good friend and a peacemaker in the midst of all the violence. In keeping

▼

with their minor roles in the plot, each of these foils is a FLAT CHAR-ACTER. Romeo—fittingly, for one of the pair of protagonists in the play—is three-dimensional in his capacities as ardent lover, reluctant defender of family honor, and loyal friend.

EXERCISES: Roles

I. Name the PROTAGONIST in *two* different NOVELS, SHORT STORIES, DRAMAS, or EPICS that you have studied recently. In each instance, give the *title* of the work, followed by the name of the character.

II. Choose *two* literary works—either those listed above or additional ones—that contain an ANTAGONIST. Identify the nature of the ANTAGONIST(s), which may be a character, a larger force, and/or a set of conflicting emotions or desires within the PROTAGONIST. For each example, explain the effects that the ANTAGONIST has on the meaning and TONE of the work.

III. Name *two* FOIL CHARACTERS in *two* literary works—either those cited in I or II above or different ones. Then explain how each character acts as a FOIL to the PROTAGONIST.

DIALOGUE

Dialogue is the presentation of what characters in a literary work say. It is a key element of DRAMA, in which, except for STAGE DIRECTIONS, dialogue makes up the entire text. It is also an important aspect of FICTION and of some NARRATIVE POETRY. Dialogue has several possible uses. It can reveal characters' motives, feelings, values, and relationships and advance the PLOT. It can also suggest TONE—that is, the speaker's attitude toward the character that he or she is addressing and the NARRATOR's attitude toward the audience.

Dialogue is a major means of depicting CHARACTER. Both the style and the content of characters' words can reveal such qualities as their relative intelligence and culture, as well as their values. The responses of other characters can suggest their relationship to one another and reveal which characters exert power over others.

In works of FICTION, the NARRATOR's commentary on the dialogue also helps shape the reader's response. In the following episode from F. Scott Fitzgerald's *The Great Gatsby*, the narrator, Nick Carraway, has just been taken by Tom Buchanan, his cousin's husband, to meet his "girl." Tom's mistress is married to the owner of a dilapidated garage, George Wilson, who has no inkling of his wife's affair. The scene that follows is Nick's—and the reader's—introduction to Wilson:

> . . . the proprietor . . . appeared in the door of an office, wiping his hands on a piece of waste. He was a blond, spiritless man, anemic, and faintly handsome. When he saw us a damp gleam of hope sprang into his light blue eyes.
>
> "Hello, Wilson, old man," said Tom, slapping him jovially on the shoulder. "How's business?"
>
> "I can't complain," answered Wilson unconvincingly. "When are you going to sell me that car?"
>
> "Next week; I've got my man working on it now."
>
> "Works pretty slow, don't he?"
>
> "No, he doesn't," said Tom coldly. "And if you feel that way about it, maybe I'd better sell it somewhere else after all."
>
> "I don't mean that," explained Wilson quickly. "I just meant—"
>
> His voice faded off and Tom glanced impatiently around the garage.

Everything about the scene implies Wilson's weakness and submission to Tom's will: his faded physical appearance, tentative gestures, and pathetic hope that Tom will bring a bit of business to the failing shop. Nick first describes him as "spiritless" and "anemic," and, fittingly, he is "wiping his hands on a bit of waste." Tom immediately takes control, speaking the first words, and "slapping" Wilson with false joviality. The one time that Wilson attempts to assert himself, Tom cuts him off "coldly," and Wilson retracts his complaint and fades into silence. The FIRST-PERSON witness leaves no doubt of the husband's powerlessness or of his betrayer's contempt.

Another technique for using dialogue to depict character is to recount differences between a character's reported thoughts and his or her spoken words. In Jane Austen's *Emma* (1816), for example, the PROTAGONIST is often prevented by the manners required in her upper-class society from expressing her actual opinions or preferences. She is skillful, though, at avoiding uncomfortable topics by maintaining a polite silence or by changing the subject. The OMNISCIENT NARRATOR reveals the contrast between Emma's thoughts and words in such comments as the following, which describes her reaction to an awkward dispute she is having with a close family friend and mentor: "It was most convenient to Emma not to make a direct reply to this assertion; she chose rather to take up her own line of the subject again."

▼

In PROSE FICTION the relative proportion of dialogue to narration varies enormously, according to the purposes of the author. Some SHORT STORIES are written almost entirely in dialogue—for example, Ernest Hemingway's "Hills Like White Elephants," a simmering quarrel between a couple at a foreign train station, in which the subject of their bitter conflict emerges only from hints in their words. Sections of NOVELS, too, are limited largely to conversation between characters, so that passages read like a short play. One example occurs in Charlotte Brontë's *Jane Eyre* (1847) during the heroine's reunion with her beloved Mr. Rochester. He is jealous of the relationship that she has had with another man, her cousin St. John Rivers, during her absence. Mr. Rochester, who has been blinded and maimed, has been severely depressed. Jane is delighted at this chance to revive his fighting spirit and direct his energies at someone who, as she knows, is no rival to him:

"How long did you reside with him and his sisters after the cousinship was discovered?"
"Five months."
"Did Rivers spend much time with the ladies of his family?"
"Yes; the back parlour was both his study and ours: he sat near the window, and we by the table."
"Did he study much?"
"A good deal."
"What?"
"Hindostanee."
"And what did you do meantime?"
"I studied German at first."
"Did he teach you?"
"He did not understand German."
"Did he teach you nothing?"
"A little Hindostanee."
"Rivers taught you Hindostanee?"
"Yes, sir."
"And his sisters also?"
"No."
"Only you?"
"Only me."
"Did you ask to learn?"
"No."
"He wished to teach you?"
"Yes."

Mr. Rochester's jealousy is implied by the cross-examination to which he subjects Jane. Knowing her intelligence and love of learning, he focuses on the role that she has played of star pupil, seeing it, rightly, as an obvious sign of Rivers's interest in Jane. His jealousy is further suggested through his concentration on the subject of their study, a rare language that suggests both Rivers's learning and his respect for Jane's abilities. It is also suggested by his pointed inquiry into whether or not Rivers singled her out from his sisters. Jane's brief answers of course pique Rochester's curiosity and tease him with the implication that she has something to hide. For the reader, the DRAMATIC IRONY is achieved by knowing Jane's actual feelings and motives. She is the NARRATOR as well as the PROTAGONIST of the novel and has confided her intentions beforehand, which makes the scene comic.

Such passages of straight dialogue may give readers the impression that they are eavesdropping on a real-life conversation, which the author has just happened to record. In actuality, the shaping hand of the writer is very much at work in such scenes. He or she chooses words and phrases that are characteristic of each speaker. The polished style eliminates the pauses, stammerings, and irrelevancies that litter everyday talk and paces the exchange for both efficiency and realism.

In addition, any contrasts between what a character says in various contexts can be both convincing and revealing. That technique is especially crucial in DRAMA, since the CHARACTERIZATION must come almost entirely through the dialogue. In Shakespeare's *Romeo and Juliet*, for example, Lord Capulet makes a series of strikingly different statements about his daughter Juliet's freedom to choose a husband. He first tells her new suitor, the County Paris, that he must "woo her" and "get her heart," for his own permission depends on her "consent." When, a short while later, Juliet has become deeply depressed, supposedly over her cousin Tybalt's death, Capulet decides that marriage would be the ideal cure for her melancholy. He tells the count that he can vouch for his daughter's agreement to an immediate wedding: "I think she will be ruled / In all respects by me; nay more, I doubt it not." Juliet, however, is grieving over her forced separation from Romeo, the son of her family's mortal enemy, whom she has secretly married. Without revealing the reason, she refuses the match with Paris. Capulet, outraged, tells her: "An you be mine, I'll give you to my friend; / An you be not, hang, beg, starve, die in the streets." Capulet's initial permissiveness, it is suggested, depended on his conviction that his daughter's will coincides with his own. His authority threatened, Capulet goes from being the indulgent parent to the ruthless tyrant. The inconsistencies in his attitude make him a more plausible, although not a more sympathetic, character.

In a NOVEL, a NOVELLA, and a SHORT STORY, the author may also shape the impact of dialogue by using **speech headings**, descriptions of characters' vocal tones or gestures as they speak a line. Some examples are the phrases "slapping him jovially on the shoulder" and "explained Wilson quickly" in the passage from *The Great Gatsby*. The authorial presence is also usually evident in descriptions of action and setting that are included with the dialogue.

In plays, such functions may be served by the **stage directions**, available to readers of the text but needing to be suggested in performance. Some playwrights are markedly spare in the stage direction that they use. Those of Shakespeare and other Renaissance dramatists, for example, are usually limited to entrances, exits, and sound effects. Any slightly more elaborate descriptions of settings and actions in the plays, implied by the dialogue, have usually been added by later editors and enclosed in square brackets. An example is the stage direction in *Hamlet* after the grief-stricken Laertes demands that the burial of his sister pause until he has "caught her once more in [his] arms": [*Leaps into the grave*].

In Shakespeare's case the reason for this sparsity was probably that he was writing primarily for performance, and for a repertory company of which he was a member. Most recent playwrights, such as Tennessee Williams, Arthur Miller, and August Wilson, tend to give much more elaborate descriptions of how they want lines to be delivered and how they intend characters to move on stage. The following set of stage directions, for example, appears in Williams's *The Glass Menagerie* in the aftermath of a quarrel between the adult son and his mother:

> *The music of "Ave Maria" is heard softly.*
>
> *Tom glances sheepishly but sullenly at her averted figure and slumps at the table.*
>
> *The coffee is scalding hot; he sips it and gasps and spits it back in the cup. At his gasp,* AMANDA *catches her breath and half turns. Then she catches herself and turns back to the window.* TOM *blows on his coffee, glancing sidewise at his mother. She clears her throat.* TOM *clears his. He starts to rise, sinks back down again, scratches his head, clears his throat again.* AMANDA *coughs.* TOM *raises his cup in both hands to blow on it, his eyes staring over the rim of it at his mother for several moments. Then he slowly sets the cup down and awkwardly and hesitantly rises from the chair.*

From the background music to the gasps and throat clearings to the awkward glances, it is clear that both parties to the quarrel care about one another and are preparing to make up.

The style of dialogue also varies considerably from work to work. Some authors of FICTION, such as Henry James and George Eliot, give characters long, elaborate speeches. Others, such as Hemingway and Salinger, are notable for the brevity and naturalness with which characters speak. DRAMA, too, shows an enormous range in degrees of FORMALITY, depending both on the period in which it was written and on the requirements of a particular scene. Even a play such as *Hamlet*, for example, written over four hundred years ago and full of famously poetic speeches, such as the "To be or not to be" SOLILOQUY, also contains lines of startling conciseness and modernity. Examples include the opening line, "Who's there?" and Hamlet's impatient demand, "Now, mother, what's the matter?"

A technique for creating lively dialogue, common to both DRAMA and prose FICTION, is **repartee** (reh-par-TEE), a rapid-fire exchange of witty remarks in which each speaker tries to score against an opponent in a verbal fencing match. Shakespeare uses repartee to depict both serious conflicts, such as Hamlet's bitter confrontation with his mother in III.4, and comic clashes between sparring couples. One example in *The Taming of the Shrew* occurs at the first meeting between the rebellious Kate and Petruchio, the man who has vowed to "tame" her:

PETRUCHIO Nay, come, Kate, come, you must not look so sour.
KATE It is my fashion when I see a crab.[1]
PETRUCHIO Why, here's no crab, and therefore look not sour.
KATE There is, there is.
PETRUCHIO Then show it me.
KATE   Had I a glass[2] I would.

It is clear from the brevity of the lines and the frankness of Kate's wit both that Petruchio will have no easy task and that the couple is well matched. Later masters of repartee include Oscar Wilde in the nineteenth century and Noel Coward, David Mamet, and Wendy Wasserstein in the twentieth.

In DRAMA, the means of access to a character's thoughts are confined to speeches that are directed at the audience. These are of two types: the SOLILOQUY and the ASIDE.

---

1. Crabapple.
2. Mirror.

► # Soliloquy

A **soliloquy** (soh-LIL-oh-kwee) is a monologue delivered by a character who is alone on stage. He or she may address the audience as though they are confidantes or simply seem to be thinking aloud, expressing thoughts that are too private or too risky to share with other characters. Soliloquies represent a break in the action and are reserved for major characters, usually the PROTAGONIST, and for important revelations. The technique was popular in English drama during the seventeenth and eighteenth centuries. Shakespeare, in particular, uses it to great effect to reveal characters' strongest convictions and deepest feelings.

Often, Shakespeare's villains, who are too sly to reveal their evil intentions to characters they are plotting against, confide in the audience. Lady Macbeth is the wife of the protagonist of *Macbeth*, a tragedy about ambition and betrayal. She first appears reading aloud a letter from her husband, a Scottish nobleman and general, who has just won a major military victory. Macbeth describes an eerie encounter he has just had with three witches, who have promised him future honor and power, including the kingship. Immediately, he receives an unexpected promotion. Calling her his "dearest partner of greatness," he urges his wife to "rejoice" at their new fortune. Lady Macbeth's reaction is expressed in a passionate soliloquy. She doubts that he possesses the mercilessness that would be needed to seize the throne by criminal means. She is eager for Macbeth to get home so that she can spur him on to greater ambition. A messenger then enters to say that the present ruler, King Duncan, is coming to stay at their castle. After she dismisses the messenger, her soliloquy continues:

> The raven[1] himself is hoarse
> That croaks the fatal entrance of Duncan
> Under my battlements. Come, you spirits
> That tend on mortal[2] thoughts, unsex me here,
> And fill me from the crown to the toe top-full   5
> Of direst cruelty. Make thick my blood,
> Stop up th'access and passage to remorse,[3]
> That no compunctious visitings of nature[4]
> Shake my fell[5] purpose, nor keep peace[6] between

---

1. A bird thought to foreshadow evil and death.
2. Accompany deadly.
3. Pity.
4. Natural feelings of sympathy.
5. Cruel.
6. Calm, appease.

Th'effect and it.[7] Come to my woman's breasts,   10
And take my milk for[8] gall, you murd'ring ministers,[9]
Wherever in your sightless substances
You wait on[10] nature's mischief. Come, thick night,
And pall thee in the dunnest[11] smoke of hell,
That my keen knife see not the wound it makes,   15
Nor heaven peep through the blanket of the dark
To cry 'Hold, hold!'

The soliloquy reveals that Lady Macbeth immediately sees the
king's visit as an opportunity to murder him: she calls his arrival
"fatal." She allies herself with the supernatural forces of evil and
calls on them in a vivid HYPERBOLE to fill her from head to toe with
"direst cruelty." She wants them to block any feeling of "remorse"
that might stir up misgivings and to destroy all elements of compassion in her. Lady Macbeth conceives of those tender feelings as feminine and weak. She goes so far as to make the horrifying demand:
"unsex me here."

She has introduced that warped conception of gender roles in the
first half of the soliloquy, when she accuses Macbeth of being "too
full o' th' milk of human kindness" to act pitilessly. The METAPHOR
compares sympathy to mother's milk, humanity's most nurturing
substance, which she scorns. Now, she demands that the "murd'ring
ministers" to whom she is praying replace the milk in her "woman's
breasts" with "gall," a bitter secretion. She also pleads for the thick-
est "smoke of hell" to cover up the act of murder even from her
own eyes, so that her "keen knife see not the wound it makes." That
PERSONIFICATION of the murder weapon is followed by another, of
"heaven" trying to stop the terrible act by crying out "'Hold, hold!'"

On the surface, the soliloquy makes Lady Macbeth seem totally
ruthless. Its very violence, however, suggests how much against her
basic nature she is acting. She is aware that she is defying the forces
of both humane feeling ("nature") and religion ("heaven"). In order to
succeed, she feels that she must destroy her own identity, as a woman,
a loyal subject, and a Christian. She is so overwhelmed by the horror
of her goals that she calls on the forces of evil to aid her not once but
three times, in the repeated APOSTROPHE "Come." She also envisions
the moment of the knife making the fatal wound in vividly specific

---

7. Keep my purpose from achieving its goal.
8. In exchange for.
9. Agents of murder.
10. Assist.
11. Envelop yourselves in the darkest.

▼

detail. Lady Macbeth will not, in fact, carry out the murder herself, but she will persuade Macbeth to do it. The soliloquy foreshadows the terrible guilt and remorse that she will suffer for so brutally suppressing the qualms of her own conscience.

The effects of a soliloquy on the audience are similar to those of FIRST-PERSON NARRATION in a SHORT STORY or a NOVEL. In both cases, the audience has to gauge the RELIABILITY—the relative credibility—of the speaker. If he or she is a villain, such as Lady Macbeth or Iago in *Othello*, the audience may feel both flattered by being taken into the confidence of so clever a schemer and disturbed or revolted by being made a sort of accessory to his or her crimes. When the motives of the **soliloquizer** are benevolent, however, as in Juliet's soliloquy expressing her conflicting ardor and shyness about consummating her secret marriage to Romeo, "Gallop apace, you fiery footed steeds," the effect is to create bonds of sympathy between speaker and audience. The equivalent of the soliloquy in modern films is the voice-over, in which the camera shows a close-up of a silent character, focusing on the changing facial expressions while the soundtrack presents his or her voice. In fact, that method is often used to stage filmed versions of Shakespearean soliloquies, for example in Laurence Olivier's performance of the "To be or not to be" soliloquy from *Hamlet*.

▶

Aside

An **aside** is a speech, usually brief, that is heard only by the audience, or, sometimes, is addressed privately to another character on stage. If only the audience hears the aside, it may be a softly spoken remark on the scene taking place, so that it represents a thought said aloud. For example, in Shakespeare's *Hamlet*, King Claudius plots to kill his stepson/nephew by poisoning his wine at a fencing match attended by the whole court. When, instead, the queen drinks the wine, Claudius knows that expressing his anguish aloud would risk revealing his treasonous scheme to the court. Therefore, he confines his reaction to a horrified aside: "It is the poisoned cup; it is too late."

An example of an aside addressed to another character occurs in Shakespeare's comedy *The Taming of the Shrew*. As part of his "taming" process, Petruchio is trying to teach his rebellious wife the ill effects of bad temper as well as to make her submit to his will. He has been throwing a tantrum over a gown that a tailor has just delivered and that Kate protests that she adores. Just before Petruchio orders the tailor to take the gown away, he says in an aside to a friend who has been watching the quarrel: "Hortensio, say thou wilt see the tailor paid." The aside lets Petruchio keep up the pose to Kate of being an iron-willed tyrant while at the same time assuring the audience that he is carrying on an elaborate farce.

EXERCISE: Dialogue

For each of the following passages:

- Indicate those instances in which the dialogue is an example of REPARTEE, a SOLILOQUY, or an ASIDE, and explain why that term applies.
- Explain the functions and effects of any NARRATIVE description, SPEECH HEADINGS, and/or STAGE DIRECTIONS.
- Explain how the style and content of the passage help to characterize the speaker or speakers.

1. *The following conversation is between the young Jane Eyre and the Reverend Mr. Brocklehurst, the proprietor of the boarding school to which she is being sent:*

   I stepped across the rug; he placed me square and straight before him. What a face he had, now that it was almost on a level with mine! What a great nose! and what a mouth! and what large prominent teeth!

   "No sight so sad as that of a naughty child," he began, "especially a naughty little girl. Do you know where the wicked go after death?"

   "They go to hell," was my ready and orthodox answer.

   "And what is hell? Can you tell me that?"

   "A pit full of fire."

   "And should you like to fall into that pit, and to be burning there for ever?"

   "No, sir."

   "What must you do to avoid it?"

   I deliberated a moment; my answer, when it did come, was objectionable: "I must keep in good health and not die."

   "How can you keep in good health? Children younger than you die daily. I buried a little child of five years old only a day or two since—a good little child, whose soul is now in heaven. It is to be feared the same could not be said of you, were you to be called hence." —CHARLOTTE BRONTÉ, *Jane Eyre*

2. *The following speakers from Shakespeare's* King Lear *are sisters who are competing for the same lover. In her previous speech, Regan has said, "Lady, I am not well."*

▼

REGAN Sick, O, sick!

GONERIL [*aside*] If not, I'll ne'er trust medicine.[1]

3. *In the following scene, set in London in the 1890s, Algernon and Jack are old friends, and Gwendolen is Jack's fiancée:*

ALGERNON Have you told Gwendolen yet that you have an excessively pretty ward who is only just eighteen?

JACK Oh! One doesn't blurt these things out to people. Cecily and Gwendolen are perfectly certain to be extremely great friends. I'll bet you anything you like that half an hour after they have met, they will be calling each other sister.

ALGERNON Women only do that when they have called each other a lot of other things first. Now, my dear boy, if we want to get a good table at Willis's, we really must go and dress. Do you know it is nearly seven?

JACK [*Irritably*] Oh! it always is nearly seven.

ALGERNON Well, I'm hungry.

JACK I never knew you when you weren't. . . .

ALGERNON What shall we do after dinner? Go to the theatre?

JACK Oh no! I loathe listening.

ALGERNON Well, let us go to the club?

JACK Oh, no! I hate talking.

ALGERNON Well, we might trot round to the Empire[2] at ten?

JACK Oh no! I can't bear looking at things. It is so silly.

ALGERNON Well, what shall we do?

JACK Nothing!

ALGERNON It is awfully hard work doing nothing. However, I don't mind hard work where there is no definite object of any kind.

—OSCAR WILDE, *The Importance of Being Earnest*

4. *Juliet, who is secretly married to Romeo, is desperate to escape a marriage that her parents have arranged to the County Paris. She has planned with her spiritual advisor, Friar Laurence, to take a potion that will make her appear dead. Once she has been laid to rest in the family vault, the Friar promises, he will bring Romeo to take her away and hide with her until the Friar can reconcile their feuding families. The following speech takes place just after Juliet has said good night to her unsuspecting Nurse and mother.*

Farewell! God knows when we shall meet again.

---

1. A euphemism for poison.

2. A music hall.

I have a faint cold fear thrills through my veins
That almost freezes up the heat of life.
I'll call them back again to comfort me.
Nurse!—What should she do here?   5
My dismal scene I needs must act alone.
Come vial.
What if this mixture do not work at all?
Shall I be married then tomorrow morning?
No, no! This shall forbid it. Lie thou there.   10
        [*Lays down a dagger.*]
What if it be a poison which the friar
Subtly hath ministered to have me dead,
Lest in this marriage he should be dishonored
Because he married me before to Romeo?
I fear it is; and yet methinks it should not,[3]   15
For he hath still been tried[4] a holy man.
How if, when I am laid into the tomb,
I wake before the time that Romeo
Come to redeem me? There's a fearful point!
Shall I not then be stifled in the vault,   20
To whose foul mouth no healthsome air breathes in,
And there die strangled ere[5] my Romeo comes?
Or, if I live, is it not very like
The horrible conceit[6] of death and night,
Together with the terror of the place—   25
As in a vault, an ancient receptacle
Where for this many hundred years the bones
Of all my buried ancestors are packed,
Where bloody Tybalt, yet but green in earth,[7]
Lies fest'ring in his shroud, where, as they say,   30
At some hours in the night spirits resort—
Alack, alack, is it not like that I,
So early waking—what with loathsome smells,
And shrieks like mandrakes[8] torn out of the earth,
That living mortals, hearing them, run mad—   35
O, if I wake, shall I not be distraught,

---

3. Should not be.
4. Always proven to be.
5. Suffocated before.
6. Very likely that the horrible conception.
7. Newly buried.
8. A plant with a forked root resembling the human body. It was believed to utter a
   shriek when pulled up that caused those who heard it to go mad.

Environèd with all these hideous fears,
And madly play with my forefathers' joints,
And pluck the mangled Tybalt from his shroud,
And, in this rage, with some great kinsman's bone   40
As with a club dash out my desp'rate brains?
O, look! Methinks I see my cousin's ghost
Seeking out Romeo, that did spit his body
Upon a rapier's point. Stay, Tybalt, stay!
Romeo, Romeo, Romeo! Here's drink. I drink to thee.   45
[*She drinks from the vial and falls upon her bed within the curtains.*]
                        —WILLIAM SHAKESPEARE, *Romeo and Juliet*

5. The next day at school I inquired among the students about jobs
    and was given the name of a white family who wanted a boy to do
    chores. That afternoon, as soon as school had let out, I went to the
    address. A tall, dour white woman talked to me. Yes, she needed a
    boy, an honest boy. Two dollars a week. Mornings, evenings, and all
    day Saturdays. Washing dishes. Chopping wood. Scrubbing floors.
    Cleaning the yard. I would get my breakfast and dinner. As I asked
    timid questions, my eyes darted about. What kind of food would I
    get? Was the place as shabby as the kitchen indicated?

    "Do you want this job?" the woman asked.

    "Yes, m'am," I said, afraid to trust my own judgment.

    "Now, boy, I want to ask you one question and I want you to
    tell me the truth," she said.

    "Yes, m'am," I said, all attention.

    "Do you steal?" she asked me seriously.

    I burst into a laugh, then checked myself.

    "What's so damn funny about that?" she asked.

    "Lady, if I was a thief, I'd never tell anybody."

    "What do you mean?" she blazed with a red face.

    I had made a mistake during my first five minutes in the white
    world. I hung my head.

    "No, m'am," I mumbled. "I don't steal."

    She stared at me, trying to make up her mind.
                        —RICHARD WRIGHT, *Black Boy*

6. *The following episode from Arthur Miller's* Death of a Salesman *occurs when
    Biff pays a surprise visit to his father, Willy, who is a traveling salesman stay-
    ing at a hotel. Biff has gone to tell him that he has failed math and will not
    graduate from high school unless Willy can persuade his teacher to bend the
    rules. Willy, who has long been married to Biff's mother, the self-sacrificing
    Linda, is not alone and has ordered the other woman to hide:*

[THE WOMAN *laughs offstage*]

BIFF Somebody got in your bathroom!

WILLY No, it's the next room, there's a party—

THE WOMAN [*Enters laughing*] Can I come in? There's something in
the bathtub, Willy, and it's moving!

[WILLY *looks at* BIFF, *who is staring open-mouthed and horrified at*
THE WOMAN]

WILLY Ah—you better go back to your room. They must be finished
painting by now. They're painting her room so I let her take a
shower here. Go back, go back . . . [*He pushes her*]

THE WOMAN [*Resisting*] But I've got to get dressed, Willy, I can't—

WILLY Get out of here! Go back, go back . . . [*Suddenly striving for
the ordinary*] This is Miss Francis, Biff, she's a buyer. They're
painting her room. Go back, Miss Francis, go back . . .

THE WOMAN But my clothes, I can't go out naked in the hall!

WILLY [*Pushing her offstage*] Get outa here! Go back, go back!

[*Biff slowly sits down on his suitcase as the argument continues
offstage*]

7. *In the following story, a family of five and their grandmother have had a
car accident on an isolated road in Tennessee. A "big battered hearse-like
automobile" has slowly driven toward them, and the driver and two boys
with him have gotten out, holding guns.*

"We've had an ACCIDENT!" the children screamed.

The grandmother had the peculiar feeling that the bespectacled
man was someone she knew. His face was as familiar to her as if she
had known him all her life but she could not recall who he was. He
moved away from the car and began to come down the embank-
ment, placing his feet carefully so that he wouldn't slip. He had on
tan and white shoes and no socks, and his ankles were red and thin.
"Good afternoon," he said. "I see you all had a little spill."

"We turned over twice!" said the grandmother.

"Oncet," he corrected. "We seen it happen. Try their car and
see will it run, Hiram," he said quietly to the boy with the gray hat.

"What you got that gun for?" John Wesley asked. "Whatcha
gonna do with that gun?"

"Lady," the man said to the children's mother, "would you mind
calling them children to sit down by you? Children make me nervous.
I want you all to sit down right together there where you're at."

"What are you telling us what to do for?" June Star asked.

Behind them the line of woods gaped like a dark open mouth.
"Come here," said their mother.

—FLANNERY O'CONNOR, "A Good Man Is Hard to Find"

► ## Setting

The **setting** is the time and place in which the events in a work of FIC-
TION, DRAMA, or NARRATIVE POETRY occur. Individual episodes within a
work may have separate, specific settings. For example, the general setting of Homer's *The Odyssey* is ancient Greece, but various episodes are
set in such places as Odysseus's native island of Ithaca, Helen and Mene-
laus's palace in Sparta, and the home of the gods on Mount Olympus.

For a work's setting, "time" may be a historical period, time of
year, and/or time of day or night. "Place" may refer to a geographi-
cal location, to a kind of building, or to a part of a larger structure,
such as a cave or a particular room. For example, the main setting
of Joseph Conrad's *Heart of Darkness* is a boat navigating the waters
of the Belgian Congo toward the end of the nineteenth century; and
Tennessee Williams's "memory play," *The Glass Menagerie*, takes
place in a shabby apartment in St. Louis during the Depression.

In some works, the setting is purely imaginary. For example,
Jonathan Swift's fantasy travelogue, *Gulliver's Travels*, is set in a
series of fictional lands, such as Lilliput, a country of tiny and petty-
minded inhabitants. J. R. R. Tolkien's Middle Earth in *The Lord of the
Rings* trilogy is a fairy tale land inhabited by such mythical creatures
as trolls and elves. Although Illyria, the setting of Shakespeare's comedy *Twelfth Night*, was the Greeks' and Romans' name for the eastern
coast of the Adriatic, in the play Illyria is an indefinite locale whose
name suggests a mixture of "illusion," "lyrical," and "Elysium." The
setting in a work may also shift back and forth between two contrasting places, such as the peaceful raft on the Mississippi River and
the strife-torn land in Mark Twain's *Adventures of Huckleberry Finn*.

As the examples above suggest, in many works, the setting is
an essential element in establishing the ATMOSPHERE. For example,
Romeo and Juliet, Shakespeare's TRAGEDY of doomed love and bitter
feuding, is set in Italy. During the Renaissance, that land was associated with passionate romance and sudden violence. The time setting in the play is also significant: mid-July, the hottest point in the
hottest season in that southern climate. The duel that sets events
on their tragic course occurs in a Verona piazza at high noon. Just
before it breaks out, the mild-mannered Benvolio tries to persuade
his rash friend Mercutio to go indoors, cautioning:

> The day is hot, the Capels[1] are abroad,
> And, if we meet, we shall not scape a brawl,
> For now, these hot days, is the mad blood stirring.

---

1. Capulets, their enemies.

In Shakespeare's *Macbeth*, in contrast, where the initial cause of the tragedy is a brutal, carefully plotted assassination, the murder takes place in an isolated chamber of a castle in the dead of night.

In the most extreme examples of this connection between setting and plot, the setting plays a more SYMBOLIC role, FIGURATIVELY reflecting the feelings and experiences of the characters. In Charlotte Brontë's *Jane Eyre*, for example, each of the locations in the PROTAGONIST'S fictional autobiography has a SYMBOLIC name. Lowood, the charity school to which the young Jane is sent, is located in a *low*-lying valley and run by a tyrannical clergyman who "would" wish to keep the social status of the poor orphans in his charge "low" and their attitude humble. Thornfield, the manor house of Jane's beloved but morally suspect Mr. Rochester, is surrounded by thorn trees and is also the site of the trials that she must undergo—"thorns" in her life—to win happiness in the end. Jane, who is also the NARRATOR, calls attention to that METAPHORICAL connection when she first arrives at Thornfield, before she has met Mr. Rochester: "Externals have a great effect on the young: I thought that a fairer era of life was beginning for me, one that was to have its flowers and pleasures, as well as its thorns and toils."

Although the connection between setting and story is not often so direct, it is usually significant. As with other aspects of NARRATION, an author's choices about time and place exert an important influence on a work's TONE and meaning, which the reader must infer. See also ATMOSPHERE and PATHETIC FALLACY.

EXERCISES: Setting

I. For each of the following descriptions of a literary work, answer the questions about the probable effects of the SETTING.

1. Jane Austen's COMIC NOVEL Emma *is* SET *in an English country village in the early nineteenth century. The* PROTAGONIST *is a privileged young woman who lives with her widowed father in a large manor house. The owner of the other large estate in town, a bachelor, is a close family friend. Another significant place in the story is the vicarage, recently occupied by a new young minister, also a bachelor. A third is the house of Emma's dear friend, and former governess, who has recently married a widower with a highly eligible son. He has been raised by wealthy relatives and, as the book opens, has never visited the village. Finally, there is a small rented flat inhabited by a kindly, talkative woman, her aged mother, and their talented, elegant*

▼

niece, who is visiting them after a stay in the resort city of Bath. The action takes place over nearly a year, beginning in the fall of one year and concluding in mid-summer of the next. What would the setting lead readers to expect about the events and the TONE of the novel?

2. Stephen Crane's SHORT STORY "The Open Boat" is SET in a small lifeboat that has escaped the sinking ship that carried it. Its passengers are four men, the captain, two of the crew, and a newspaper correspondent who had been a passenger on the ship. During the long day and night that the story describes, the men's survival depends on continuously bailing out the leaky boat and, at the same time, trying to navigate the enormous waves that threaten every moment to capsize them. The captain has been injured, and the other three men are obliged to share the hard rowing duties. They are also threatened by an attack from a circling shark, and they are dismayed when they get within sight of land but find the surf too strong to allow them to row ashore. The men achieve a "subtle brotherhood" as they strive to survive. How might the SETTING influence the CHARACTERIZATION of the men and the TONE of the story?

3. Henrik Ibsen's PLAY A Doll's House is set in a prosperous middle-class home in Oslo, Norway, near the end of the nineteenth century. In that period women's rights were severely restricted and a wife was expected to defer to her husband's authority. The PROTAGONIST, Nora Helmer, has largely played the dutiful role prescribed by her society, and her husband has treated her like a favorite child. She has secretly rebelled against that role, however, by taking out an illegal loan and forging her late father's signature, since women were not allowed to borrow money on their own. The loan was to finance a trip to a warmer climate for her husband, then seriously ill, which his doctor had recommended as necessary for saving his life. The cure worked, and Nora is proud of her initiative and determination. As the play opens, however, the holder of the loan is threatening to expose the forgery, and Nora fears that her husband loves her so much that he will take the blame for her action and ruin his own reputation. She discovers, to her shock, that he is instead concerned only about the effect on his public image. She realizes that she has never really known him, and she makes the radical decision to leave him. How might the SETTING, in time of the historical period and in place of the Helmers' house, affect the meaning and TONE of the play?

II.

- Specify the SETTING in time and place of two works of FICTION, DRAMA, or NARRATIVE POETRY that you have read. Note: A work may have multiple settings within the larger one. Include those that are most significant.

- Describe the effects that the time and place in which the work is SET have on the work's meaning and TONE.

III.

- Describe *one* work of literature that contains two strongly contrasting SETTINGS.
- Explain how that contrast in time and place affects the work's meaning and TONE.

Theme ◀

The **theme** of a literary work is a central idea that it conveys, either directly or by implication. In its broad sense, the term refers to a concept that recurs in many works of literature—for example, courtship, the horrors of war, or conflict between parents and children. The narrower meaning of theme is a view or a value conveyed by a particular literary work. The theme differs from the subject of the work, a neutral summary of the characters and events, and instead expresses a moral or philosophical stance toward the subject. For example, the subject of Charlotte Brontë's *Jane Eyre* is an orphan girl's growth to womanhood in nineteenth-century England. The novel's themes include the importance of being true to one's values and the power of romantic love.

Some authors' themes are asserted openly, especially in works whose major purpose is to instruct or persuade. For example, Alexander Pope's poem "An Essay on Man" is meant to teach such principles as morality and religious faith. To cite a sample passage:

Hope humbly, then; with trembling pinions soar;
Wait the great teacher Death, and God adore!
What future bliss, he gives thee not to know,
But gives that hope to be thy blessing now.

Other examples of works that state their themes directly are plays by such dramatists as Henrik Ibsen and George Bernard Shaw, which focus on themes like the rights of women and the evils of war, and satires such as George Orwell's *Animal Farm*, which exposes the tyranny and hypocrisy of totalitarianism.

In most works, however, a theme emerges by implication and is conveyed by the choices that the author makes about the NARRATION and the TONE. For example, one of the themes of Mark Twain's *Adventures of Huckleberry Finn* is that true morality depends on sympathy for

▼

others' suffering rather than on rules of conduct imposed by society or organized religion. That idea is never stated outright. Instead, it is suggested by the characters, kindly and corrupt, that the naïve, good-hearted narrator encounters. Recognizing a theme can help readers to compare and contrast works that treat the same central concept and to understand the values and attitudes that underlie a given work. At the same time, it is important to keep in mind that simply summing up the themes of complex poems, plays, and novels cannot yield their full meaning and literary power.

TONE

Tone means the attitude that a literary speaker expresses toward his or her subject matter and audience. The term is derived from speech, in which listeners note a speaker's tone of voice in order to gauge his feelings about the topic and about his relationship to his audience. Tone is described in adjectives that express emotion or manner. It may be compassionate or judgmental, scornful or reverent, formal or casual, arrogant or insecure, serious or ironic, angry or serene, confident or timid. It may remain consistent, or it may change at some point. In conversation, we receive clues to tone from the speaker's facial expressions, gestures, and vocal inflections. In written works, tone must be inferred from such factors as the SYN-TAX, DICTION, POINT OF VIEW, and SELECTION OF DETAILS.

If the passage is a DIALOGUE, in either a DRAMA, a work of PROSE FICTION, or a NARRATIVE POEM, the listener as well as the speaker is present. Therefore the reader is able to witness directly the effects and implications of speakers' words. In Shakespeare's *Twelfth Night*, the Countess Olivia has fallen in love with a young servant. He has been sent to court her for another, a duke who is of her own high class and therefore a more suitable match. Before she confesses, she apologizes for her forwardness in hinting at her passion and pays a compliment to the messenger's intelligence: "To one of your receiving [understanding, perception] / Enough is shown." In a delicious instance of DRAMATIC IRONY, however, the audience knows what Olivia does not: that the messenger is not the attractive boy he looks to be but a young woman in disguise. To further complicate the situation, the messenger, whose name is Viola, has fallen in love with the very duke whom Olivia so firmly rejects. The dialogue continues:

OLIVIA So let me hear you speak.
VIOLA I pity you.
OLIVIA   That's a degree to[1] love.
VIOLA No, not a grece,[2] for 'tis a vulgar proof[3]
    That very oft we pity enemies.

Olivia's initial tone is humble and hopeful. It is reflected in her brief lines and simple DICTION. She asks for the "boy's" reaction to her declaration. Then she eagerly tries to put the best face on his answer, completing his BLANK VERSE line with her response. Viola's tone begins as compassionate. Her parallel situation of being in love with someone who does not requite her feelings makes her "pity" Olivia. She too speaks in the simplest style. As soon as she realizes that Olivia has mistaken her sympathy for love, however, her SYNTAX turns complex and her tone commanding. As in this case, a speaker's tone may shift in the course of a scene, an important signal of changing feelings and motives.

If the speaker in question is the NARRATOR of a literary work, he or she has an implied audience, in either the reader or some invented listener. In that case, the reader must infer the narrator's attitude toward the audience. Does the narrator seem to suggest that they share the same assumptions and values?

A FIRST-PERSON NARRATOR may be UNRELIABLE, that is, biased, deceptive, or naïve. In such cases, the tone that he or she takes is meant to be seen as exaggerated or misleading. Charlotte Perkins Gilman's short story "The Yellow Wallpaper" opens with what seems at first to be a cheerful, even enraptured tone. The verb tense is present, and the reader is led to experience the events along with the protagonist/narrator:

> It is very seldom that mere ordinary people like John and myself secure ancestral halls for the summer.
>
> A colonial mansion, a hereditary estate, I would say a haunted house and reach the height of romantic felicity—but that would be asking too much of fate!
>
> Still I will proudly declare that there is something queer about it.
>
> Else, why should it be let so cheaply? And why have stood so long untenanted?
>
> John laughs at me, of course, but one expects that.
>
> John is practical in the extreme. He has no patience with

---

1. Toward.
2. Step.
3. Commonplace.

faith, an intense horror of superstition, and he scoffs openly at any talk of things not to be felt and seen and put down in figures.

John is a physician, and *perhaps*—(I would not say it to a living soul, of course, but this is dead paper and a great relief to my mind)—*perhaps* that is one reason I do not get well faster.

You see he does not believe I am sick!

And what can one do?

If a physician of high standing, and one's own husband, assures friends and relatives that there is really nothing the matter with one but temporary nervous depression—a slight hysterical tendency—what is one to do?

At first, the narrator focuses on the "colonial mansion" that she and her husband have rented, and their seemingly light disagreement about it. She is charmed by the possibility that the estate is a "haunted house," a situation she calls "the height of romantic felicity." She contrasts her attitude with that of her husband, John, who "laughs at" her fascination, adding wryly, "one expects that" in marriage. He is "practical in the extreme" and openly scornful of religious "faith," "superstition," and anything that cannot be "felt and seen and put down in figures." At this point, the narrator reveals two key points of information: John is "a physician" and she is ill, though she does not yet specify the nature of her sickness. She does, however, twice offer the opinion that "*perhaps*" his profession and his skepticism are why she does not "get well faster." Her timidity about disagreeing with his supposed expertise is suggested by the fact that the "perhaps" is both italicized and repeated. In the midst of this hesitant admission, she also describes her relief at being able to express her feelings, at least on paper. That admission suggests her fear of her husband's disapproval and her unwillingness to subject him to public criticism: she "would not say [this] to a living soul." She adds further emphasis to that statement with the "of course," as though that inferior role were the only possible lot of wives.

At the same time that she seems to be supporting that opinion, however, she shows underlying disagreement by admitting to the reader that writing down this accusation against John provides "a great relief to [her] mind." She assures herself that no harm will be done to him by her frankness, since her audience is "dead paper." That is a poignant indication of her self-defeating wish to protect the husband whose cold and judgmental nature may be at the root of her illness. He, a "physician," should be a source of comfort and healing. Instead, his rejection of the spiritual/imaginative aspects of human consciousness undermines his wife's emotional health.

In mid-passage, she states her dilemma more explicitly, again turning to the reader for understanding: "You see he does not believe I am sick!" Then she asks a RHETORICAL QUESTION that sums up her feeling of helplessness: "And what can one do?" She notes the odds against her: John is "a physician of high standing" and her "own husband." She also reveals the psychological nature of her illness, which he labels a "temporary nervous depression," a "slight hysterical tendency."

The impression established by the story's opening is of a quietly desperate woman. She is oppressed by a husband whose male chauvinist convictions and condescending attitude are aggravating her nervous depression. She is unable or unwilling fully to admit the extent of the harm that he is doing her. The refrains in her narrative, however—"John says" and "what is one to do?"—suggest both her emotional imprisonment and her anguished loneliness. Her only confidants are the "dead paper" on which she writes and the reader to whom she appeals for understanding.

A THIRD-PERSON NARRATOR, whether INTRUSIVE or OBJECTIVE, may adopt a tone that seems factual and neutral. A surface attitude of objectivity, however, may imply an underlying meaning at odds with that tone, creating VERBAL IRONY. For example, Franz Kafka's "A Hunger Artist" opens with what seems to be a brief history of a popular entertainment:

> During these last decades the interest in professional fasting has markedly diminished. It used to pay very well to stage such great performances under one's own management, but today that is quite impossible. We live in a different world now.

The first line is on the surface a matter-of-fact assertion about the art's fading popularity. It is only when the reader reconsiders the phrase that describes the practice—"professional fasting"—that the discrepancy between the narrator's straightforward tone and the bizarre subject matter hits home. The account goes on from the point of view of a promoter of this so-called spectator sport. He comments on how profitable it once was to stage a fast. Then he complains about the change that has taken place in the public's interest. "We live in a different world now," the OMNISCIENT NARRATOR pronounces regretfully. The grotesquely inappropriate enthusiasm for this form of suffering signals the IRONIC tone. The irony is also implied by the fact that nothing usually associated with "art" is achieved by the performance—no beauty of movement or visible product. It simply has the same effect as a wasting disease, so that it should inspire revulsion and horror. Because the narrator's tone completely lacks those feelings, the shock for the reader, and therefore the irony, are redoubled.

A narrative may, in contrast, create **pathos** (PAY-thohss), the evocation in the audience of pity, tenderness, or sorrow. In nineteenth-century fiction, pathos was a frequent feature of death scenes, particularly those describing children, such as Paul Dombey in Charles Dickens's *Dombey and Son* and Beth in Louisa May Alcott's *Little Women*. To modern readers, such scenes may seem too sentimental. Pathos that depends instead on UNDERSTATEMENT is often seen as subtler and therefore more moving. The protagonist of James Joyce's "Clay" is the tiny, elderly Maria, who works as a kitchen maid in a charitable institution for fallen women. Maria is cheerful and uncomplaining—her favorite word is "nice." The story is set on All Hallows Eve (Halloween), and she is looking forward to her annual visit with the family of a man she once worked for as a nanny. In keeping with the Irish holiday tradition, they play a fortune-telling game, which involves being blindfolded and choosing an object that predicts one's future. A ring means marriage, a prayer book entrance to a convent. In this passage, Maria is serving the women their tea, her last task before her evening out:

> There was a great deal of laughing and joking during the meal. Lizzie Fleming said Maria was sure to get the ring and though Fleming had said that for so many Hallow Eves, Maria had to laugh and say she didn't want any ring or man either; and when she laughed her grey-green eyes sparkled with disappointed shyness and the tip of her nose nearly met the tip of her chin.

The suggestion of how much Maria would have wished to marry and have a family is suggested by the "disappointed shyness" that she covers with her exaggerated laugh. The description of her witchlike features, ironically at odds with her kindly nature, hints at why Maria has never found love.

The pathos is increased when, at the party, some girls play a cruel joke and add clay from the backyard to Maria's choices. In polite versions of the game, clay is omitted because it symbolizes death. The adults are furious at the girls' insensitivity. Maria, however, still blindfolded, has no idea what has caused the commotion. The THIRD-PERSON LIMITED NARRATOR takes us into her childlike perspective: "Maria understood that it was wrong that time and so she had to do it over again: and this time she got the prayer-book." The next morning, a mass day for which the pious Maria has set her alarm clock an hour early, is All Saints' Day. Joyce has suggested Maria's fate, as well as her naïve unawareness of the harshness of her life, with touchingly understated pathos.

EXERCISES: Theme and Tone

I. For each of the following passages:
- Describe the TONE.
- Explain the aspects of the passage's DICTION, SYNTAX, POINT OF VIEW, and SELECTION OF DETAILS that help to convey that TONE.

1. Gr-r-r—there go, my heart's abhorrence!
       Water your damned flower-pots, do!
   If hate killed men, Brother Lawrence,
       God's blood, would not mine kill you!
   What? Your myrtle-bush wants trimming?   5
       Oh, that rose has prior claims—
   Needs its leaden vase filled brimming?
       Hell dry you up with its flames!
                                   –ROBERT BROWNING, "Soliloquy of the Spanish Cloister"

2. The man . . . banged his fist on the table and shouted:
       —What's for my dinner?
       —I'm going . . . to cook it, pa, said the little boy.
       —On that fire! You let the fire out! By God, I'll teach you to do
   that again!
       He took a step to the door and seized the walking-stick which
   was standing behind it.
       —I'll teach you to let the fire out! he said, rolling up his sleeve
   in order to give his arm free play.
       The little boy cried O, pa! and ran whimpering round the table,
   but the man followed and caught him by the coat. The little boy
   looked about him wildly but, seeing no way of escape, fell upon his
   knees.
       —Now, you'll let the fire out the next time! Take that, you little
   whelp!
       The boy uttered a squeal of pain as the stick cut his thigh. He
   clasped his hands together in the air and his voice shook with fright.
       —O, pa! he cried. Don't beat me, pa! And I'll . . . I'll say a *Hail
   Mary*[1] for you. . . . I'll say a *Hail Mary* for you, pa, if you don't beat
   me. . . . I'll say a *Hail Mary* . . .
                                   –JAMES JOYCE, "Counterparts"

---

1. A Catholic prayer to the Virgin Mary.

3. *In Shakespeare's* King Lear, *the old king speaks these words over the body of his daughter Cordelia, who has been hanged and lies dead in his arms:*

And my poor fool[2] is hanged! No, no, no life!
Why should a dog, a horse, a rat, have life,
And thou no breath at all? Thou'lt come no more,
Never, never, never, never, never!

4. Is this a holy thing to see,
In a rich and fruitful land,
Babes reduc'd to misery,
Fed with cold and usurous hand?

   Is that trembling cry a song?   5
   Can it be a song of joy?
   And so many children poor?
   It is a land of poverty!

                              –WILLIAM BLAKE, "Holy Thursday [II]"

II. Summarize a major THEME in two DRAMAS, SHORT STORIES, or NOVELS that you have recently studied.

---

2. A term of endearment, used here of Cordelia.

Structure

The **structure** of a literary work is its basic framework, the principles and the patterns on which it is organized. The structure may be based on the **conventions**—typical traits—of a certain form. Some examples are the five-act format of an Elizabethan tragedy, or the OCTAVE/SESTET division of an ITALIAN SONNET. Alternatively, the structure may evolve as an individual work takes shape, creating what the critic and poet Samuel Taylor Coleridge called "organic form."

Coleridge's poem "Frost at Midnight," for example, is ordered partly by its BLANK VERSE form, the steady beat of the UNRHYMED IAMBIC PENTAMETER lines. But other aspects of its style make it seem like a spontaneous expression of the NARRATOR's feelings that is unique to this poem. Those include the irregular length of the stanzas, the many exclamations, and the long enjambments. They are used to express the NARRATOR's memories of his frustrating childhood, hopes for his newborn son, and love of the beauty and power of nature. Both influences on the poem serve the major purposes of structure: to make the parts interdependent and give the whole unity.

Readers need to be alert to both the typical patterns of organization and to the techniques that create the structure of an individual work. Those factors include the order in which the story is told—whether it begins at the chronological beginning or plunges into that narrative at some later point, IN MEDIAS RES. Another factor is the focus of the narrative—whether it concentrates on a single plot and set of characters or includes a SUBPLOT, a secondary story that parallels or contrasts with the main one. A good deal of the art of narration involves aspects of the structure.

In Medias Res

One technique that has been both a convention of some forms and a special device in many works is *in medias res* (in MAY-dee-ass rayss). It means beginning a narration not in chronological order, with the first event in the plot, but at some later point. An example of a chronological opening is Edgar Allan Poe's poem "The Raven." The first lines begin with the first event in the story:

> Once upon a midnight dreary, while I pondered, weak and
> weary,
> Over many a quaint and curious volume of forgotten lore—

> While I nodded, nearly napping, suddenly there came a tapping,
> As of some one gently rapping, rapping at my chamber door—

What follows, as these lines promise, is the narrator's step-by-step account of how the mysterious bird has affected his life. A poem that begins *in medias res*, in contrast, is John Donne's "The Canonization," which begins with the demand: "For God's sake hold your tongue, and let me love." That abrupt challenge creates immediacy and surprise, advantages of the *in medias res* technique. It also imposes an obligation on the author, however. He has to go back in the story and fill in the essential background information—the **exposition**—that will allow the reader to understand the characters and the events that have been introduced.

The *in medias res* beginning is a convention of the EPIC form. For example, Homer's *Odyssey* does not open when the hero sets out from the Greeks' triumph in the Trojan War to return to his native island. Instead, it starts near the end of his almost ten-year journey, when he is marooned on the island of the nymph Calypso. It is not until a third of the way into the EPIC that the audience learns how Odysseus came to be denied the swift return to home and family for which he longs. Homer's EXPOSITION takes the form of the **flashback**, the dramatization of scenes set earlier in a story, when Odysseus relates his adventures to the hospitable Phaeacians, in books 7–12. During those books, the eloquent PROTAGONIST assumes the role of the minstrel, the epic NARRATOR whose role is to glorify the hero by telling of his extraordinary feats. Since Homer's day, the flashback has been used in countless works of fiction, drama, and film. For example, in Arthur Miller's *Death of a Salesman*, it consists of staging the PROTAGONIST'S memories and delusions, which alternate with the realistic scenes set in the present.

Another means of providing EXPOSITION is to have either the NARRATOR or a character summarize necessary background information. For example, in Jane Austen's *Emma*, each new character is introduced with a summary of his or her family origins, relationships, and sometimes, as in the passage below, physical appearance. That approach is typical of the INTRUSIVE THIRD-PERSON OMNISCIENT NARRATOR.

> Harriet Smith was the natural[1] daughter of somebody. Somebody had placed her, several years back, at Mrs. Goddard's school, and Somebody had lately raised her from the condition of scholar to that of parlour-boarder. This was all that was generally known of her history. She had no visible friends but what had been

---

1. Illegitimate.

acquired at Highbury, and was now just returned from a long visit in the country to some young ladies who had been at school there with her.

She was a very pretty girl, and her beauty happened to be of a sort which Emma particularly admired. She was short, plump and fair, with a fine bloom, blue eyes, light hair, regular features, and a look of great sweetness; and before the end of the evening, Emma was as much pleased with her manners as her person, and quite determined to continue the acquaintance.

This description occurs on the occasion of the first meeting between Harriet and Emma, the aristocratic heroine. The matchmaking Emma is looking for a new project to occupy her idle hours. Both the difference in their social status and Harriet's sweet naïveté foreshadow the uneven course that the young women's friendship will take.

Shakespeare is especially skillful at using various means of SHOWING to introduce the EXPOSITION. He interweaves facts about past conflicts, family relationships, and current issues into the action. *Romeo and Juliet*, for example, does not begin with the lovers but with the servants of the feuding families. The Capulet servants joke with each other and boast about their courage and fighting skill. Then, when a pair of Montague servants enter, they try to provoke a quarrel. As soon as the noblemen in each family arrive, the quarrel becomes an outright brawl. In addition to being exciting, the scene establishes how widespread the feud is, since even the servants are drawn into it. The EXPOSITION also suggests how threatening this violent ATMOSPHERE will be to the love relationship.

As the last example suggests, *in medias res* has been used effectively in works that, unlike the EPIC, do not depend on it as a CONVENTION of the form. Writers of FICTION, as well as DRAMA, have made extensive use of the technique. For example, James Joyce's SHORT STORY "Eveline" begins:

> She sat at the window watching the evening invade the avenue. Her head was leaned against the window curtains and in her nostrils was the odour of dusty cretonne.[2] She was tired.

It is several paragraphs before we learn that the PROTAGONIST is trying to decide whether or not to leave her dreary home and elope to Buenos Aires with a kindly sailor who has proposed to her. The passive voice of the sentences—not "she leaned her head" but "her head was leaned"—suggests her weary, defeated attitude. She is not exerting

---

2. A heavy unglazed cotton fabric, colorfully printed.

the energy even to breathe: the dusty odour was "in her nostrils." The THIRD-PERSON LIMITED POINT OF VIEW reflects not only Eveline's outlook but also her voice. It SHOWS rather than TELLS her timid, passive nature and foreshadows the story's sad outcome.

Subplot

In addition to decisions about where a narrative will begin, authors also make other key choices about its structure. A work may have only a single unified plot, or it may abruptly shift focus to a different set of characters or a new location. The drama of Shakespeare's day, for example, is full of **subplots**, secondary stories that parallel or contrast with the main action. The characters in a subplot may have a major impact on those in the main plot, or they may simply mirror some aspect of it. In Shakespeare's COMEDY *A Midsummer Night's Dream*, the main plot involving the loves of the noble couples is entirely separate from the subplot of the workmen, the "rude mechanicals," who are rehearsing a play that they hope to perform at court. At the same time, the workmen's play, a crude version of the tragedy of "Pyramus and Thisbe," concerns the same theme of separated lovers as the main plot, though in ridiculous form. A second subplot involves supernatural characters, the fairy king and queen and their servants. Only they are aware of the characters in the other plots. When the two sets of human beings enter the woods, the fairies' realm, and the characters from the three plot strands intermix, comic chaos results. The effects of the fairies' magical intervention are to mock the concepts of love at first sight and the lover's blindness to the beloved's faults. The maiden who has been the object of both young men's desires is made to change places with the young woman who had been rejected by both. Also, the delicate fairy queen is smitten with Bottom the weaver, who has been transformed into an ass. By the end, a combination of the fairy king's magic and the ruling duke's generosity restores order and brings all three plots to a happy resolution.

In Shakespeare's TRAGEDY *King Lear*, the subplot is much more closely intertwined with the main story. Two elderly noblemen, Lear himself and the Earl of Gloucester, have adult children. In each case, the father puts his trust in the treacherous child and rejects the loyal one, who has in the past been his favorite. Both fathers suffer the consequences of those misplaced affections. In other ways, however, the subplots differ. Lear has three daughters, Gloucester two sons. Lear's loyal child is his youngest, Gloucester's his elder son. Lear's daughters are legitimate and born of the same mother. Gloucester's younger son is illegitimate, the product of an adulterous affair. He is deeply resentful of his father's public mockery of him and of his virtual banishment from the kingdom. The stories converge as the villainous children form a conspiracy against their fathers that drives Lear to madness and leaves Gloucester blind and, literally, heartbroken. Lear's treacherous daughters die by murder and suicide, and his youngest is killed by one of her sisters' henchmen. Her death causes Lear's heart, like Gloucester's, to break. The earl's treacherous son repents at the end, after losing a duel to his brother, and the last of Gloucester's line goes on to inherit the throne. It is he who makes the solemn statement at the end that "the oldest hath borne most." That claim is reinforced by the fathers' movingly interwoven tragedies.

A NOVEL, too, may shift among various subplots. George Eliot's *Middlemarch* (1872), for example, traces the fortunes of several couples as they meet, court, and marry: the idealistic young Dorothea Brooke and the sour old scholar, Mr. Casaubon; Dorothea's lighthearted sister, Cecilia, and the earnest nobleman, Sir James Chettam; the ambitious medical researcher and doctor, Lydgate, and the self-centered beauty Rosamond Vincy; and Rosamond's impulsive and extravagant brother, Fred Vincy, and the practical, responsible Mary Garth. Many other long novels have multiple subplots, for example, Harriet Beecher Stowe's *Uncle Tom's Cabin* (1852), Charles Dickens's *Our Mutual Friend* (1864), Leo Tolstoy's *War and Peace* (1869), E. M. Forster's *A Passage to India* (1924), and Zadie Smith's *White Teeth* (2000).

EXERCISES: Structure

I. Each of the following passages opens a NOVEL, SHORT STORY, PLAY, or NARRATIVE POEM.

- Explain whether the work is STRUCTURED so as to begin in chronological order or *in medias res*.
- Describe how that way of beginning the work affects the meaning and the TONE.

1. True! Nervous—very, very dreadfully nervous I had been and am; but why *will* you say that I am mad? The disease had sharpened my

▼

senses—not destroyed—not dulled them. Above all things was the sense of hearing acute. I heard all things in the heaven and in the earth. I heard many things in hell. How, then, am I mad? Hearken! And observe how healthily—how calmly I can tell you the whole story. —EDGAR ALLAN POE, "The Tell-Tale Heart"

2. It is a truth universally acknowledged, that a single man in possession of a good fortune, must be in want of a wife.

   However little known the feelings or views of such a man may be on his first entering a neighborhood, this truth is so well fixed in the minds of the surrounding families, that he is considered as the rightful property of some one or other of their daughters.
   —JANE AUSTEN, *Pride and Prejudice*

3. *Enter* BERNARDO *and* FRANCISCO, *two sentinels.*
   Location: A guard platform at Elsinore Castle, Denmark.

   BERNARDO Who's there?
   FRANCISCO Nay, answer me. Stand and unfold[1] yourself.
   BERNARDO Long live the king!
   FRANCISCO   Bernardo?
   BERNARDO   He.
   FRANCISCO You come most carefully upon your hour.
   BERNARDO 'Tis now struck twelve. Get thee to bed, Francisco.   5
   FRANCISCO For this relief much thanks. 'Tis bitter cold,
                And I am sick at heart.
   BERNARDO   Have you had quiet guard?
   FRANCISCO Not a mouse stirring.
   BERNARDO   Well, good night.
                If you do meet Horatio and Marcellus,
                The rivals[2] of my watch, bid them make haste.   10
                —WILLIAM SHAKESPEARE, *Hamlet*

4. My father's family name being Pirrip, and my Christian name Phillip, my infant tongue could make of both names nothing longer or more explicit than Pip. So, I called myself Pip, and came to be called Pip.

   I give Pirrip as my father's family name, on the authority of his tombstone and my sister—Mrs. Joe Gargery, who married the blacksmith. As I never saw my father or my mother, and never saw any likeness of them (for their days were long before the days of photographs), my first fancies regarding what they were like, were

---

1. Identify.
2. Partners.

unreasonably derived from their tombstones. The shape of the letters on my father's, gave me an odd idea that he was a square, stout, dark man, with curly black hair. From the character and turn of the inscription, '*Also Georgiana Wife of the Above,*' I drew a childish conclusion that my mother was freckled and sickly. To five little stone lozenges,[3] each about a foot and a half long, which were arranged in a neat row beside their grave, and were sacred to the memory of five little brothers of mine—who gave up trying to get a living, exceedingly early in that universal struggle—I am indebted for a belief I religiously entertained that they had all been born on their backs with their hands in their trousers-pockets, and had never taken them out in this state of existence.

–CHARLES DICKENS, *Great Expectations*

5. It is an ancient Mariner
   And he stoppeth one of three,
   —"By thy long gray beard and glittering eye,
   Now wherefore stopp'st thou me?

   The Bridegroom's doors are opened wide,   5
   And I am next of kin;
   The guests are met, the feast is set:
   May'st hear the merry din."

   He holds him with his skinny hand,
   "There was a ship," quoth he.   10
   "Hold off! unhand me, graybeard loon!"
   Eftsoons[4] his hand dropped he.

   He holds him with his glittering eye—
   The wedding guest stood still,
   And listens like a three years' child: 15
   The Mariner hath his will

–SAMUEL TAYLOR COLERIDGE,
"The Rime of the Ancient Mariner"

---

3. Slabs.
4. Immediately.

▼

II. For one of the following passages:

- Explain whether the technique for providing EXPOSITION is a FLASHBACK or a narrative summary.
- Describe how that technique affects the meaning and the TONE of the passage.

1. The last time I talked to my mother, I remember I was restless. I wanted to get out and see Isabel. We weren't married then and we had a lot to straighten out between us.

    There Mama sat, in black, by the window. She was humming an old tune, *Lord, you brought me from a long ways off.* Sonny was out somewhere. Mama kept watching the streets.

    "I don't know," she said, "if I'll ever see you again, after you go off from here. But I hope you'll remember the things I tried to teach you."

    "Don't talk like that," I said, and smiled. "You'll be here a long time yet."

    She smiled, too, but she said nothing. She was quiet for a long time. And I said, "Mama, don't worry about nothing. I'll be writing all the time, and you'll be getting the checks. . . . "

    "I want to talk to you about your brother," she said, suddenly. "If anything happens to me he ain't going to have nobody to look out for him."

    "Mama," I said, "ain't nothing going to happen to you *or* Sonny. Sonny's all right. He's a good boy and he's got good sense."

    "It ain't a question of his being a good boy," Mama said, "nor of his having good sense. It ain't only the bad ones, nor yet the dumb ones that gets sucked under." She stopped, looking at me. "Your Daddy once had a brother," she said, and she smiled in a way that made me feel she was in pain. "You didn't never know that, did you?"

    "No," I said, "I never knew that," and I watched her face.

    —JAMES BALDWIN, "Sonny's Blues"

2. There was a good deal of fussing to be done before Mr. Summers declared the lottery open. There were the lists to make up—of heads of families, heads of households in each family, members of each household in each family. There was the proper swearing-in of Mr. Summers by the postmaster, as the official of the lottery; at one time, some people remembered, there had been a recital of some sort, performed by the official of the lottery, a perfunctory, tuneless chant that had been rattled off duly each year; some people believed

▼

that the official of the lottery used to stand just so when he said or sang it, others believed that he was supposed to walk among the people, but years and years ago this part of the ritual had been allowed to lapse. There had been, also, a ritual salute, which the official of the lottery had had to use in addressing each person who came up to draw from the box, but this also had changed with time, until now it was felt necessary only for the official to speak to each person approaching. Mr. Summers was very good at all this; in his clean white shirt and blue jeans, with one hand resting carelessly on the black box, he seemed very proper and important as he talked interminably to Mr. Graves and the Martins.

–SHIRLEY JACKSON, "The Lottery"

III.

- Name one NOVEL or DRAMA that you have read that contains a SUBPLOT.
- Explain how the SUBPLOT parallels or contrasts with the main PLOT and how it contributes to the meaning of the work as a whole.

Syntax

Syntax is sentence structure. It includes the sequence and connection of the words, phrases, and clauses that make up the sentences in a work. A **sentence** in English contains a **subject** and a **predicate** and can stand alone as a grammatical unit, or **independent clause**. A **dependent clause** is a group of words that contains a subject and a predicate but cannot stand alone as a grammatical unit. In order to form a sentence, it must be combined with an INDEPENDENT CLAUSE. A **phrase** is a group of words that lacks a subject, a predicate, or both, and that functions as a part of speech, such as a noun, an adverb, or an adjective.

The subject designates who or what the sentence is about. The **simple subject** is a noun or a pronoun. The **complete subject** consists of the simple subject and all of its modifiers. In the following sentences, the simple subject is underlined, and the complete subject is italicized:

> <u>Mercutio</u> loves to talk.
>
> *The <u>intensity</u> of Romeo's love for Juliet* never flags.
>
> *The main <u>goal</u> that drives Odysseus* is to reach his homeland of Ithaca.

The **predicate** is the part of the sentence that acts upon, describes, or is performed by the subject. The **simple predicate** is the **verb**—the word that signifies an action or a state of being. The **complete predicate** consists of the verb and all of its modifiers, objects, and complements. In the following sentences, the simple predicate is underlined, and the complete predicate is italicized:

> The rain *<u>fell</u>*.
>
> Jane Eyre *<u>flees</u> from Thornfield in a state of panic.*
>
> Benvolio *<u>is</u> loyal to Romeo throughout the play.*

In addition to the subject and the predicate, a sentence may contain one or more additional elements.

- A **direct object**, which completes the predicate by indicating who or what receives the action expressed by the verb:

> Jane draws *a portrait* of Mr. Rochester.
>
> Gatsby loves *Daisy Buchanan.*

- An **indirect object**, which is a noun or a pronoun that indicates to whom or for whom an action is done:

Juliet sends a ring *to Romeo*.

Orlando writes *Rosalind* several verses.

- An **appositive**, a noun or a noun phrase that describes or equates with a nearby noun or pronoun:

Holden, *an affectionate brother*, enjoys Phoebe's company.

An unscrupulous thief, he exploits young Oliver Twist.

Sentence Fragments

In English, sentences are indicated by beginning the first word with a capital letter and placing an end mark such as a period after the last word. A sentence that is so punctuated but that lacks either a subject, a predicate, or both is called a **sentence fragment**. For example, the fragment "*Did, too*" lacks a subject. The fragment "*A huge wave*" lacks a predicate. The fragment "*On the corner of the street*"—a prepositional phrase because it begins with a preposition—lacks both a subject and a predicate. An unintentional sentence fragment disrupts the sense of a sentence and, in formal style, is a grammatical error. Writers sometimes use fragments deliberately, however. One reason is to create believable, casual dialogue. The following passage from Tillie Olsen's SHORT STORY "Tell Me a Riddle" uses three sentence fragments in a row to capture the impatient voice of a sick old woman:

"A babbler. All my life around babblers. Enough!"

An intentional sentence fragment can also create emphasis. In the following passage, the NARRATOR of Alice Walker's "Everyday Use," a concerned mother, is making an effort to understand her ambitious daughter. She makes a brief statement, and then uses two long sentence fragments to specify past examples of her daughter's enterprising character:

Dee wanted nice things. A yellow organdy dress to wear to her graduation from high school; black pumps to match a green suit she'd made from an old suit somebody gave me.

Kinds of Sentences

Sentences may be classified in several ways.

- The **simple sentence** consists of a single INDEPENDENT CLAUSE:

  Jane rebels.

  Jay Gatsby gives lavish parties.

  Tybalt, driven by his hatred of the Montagues, provokes the fatal duel.

- The **compound sentence** contains more than one INDEPENDENT CLAUSE, with no SUBORDINATE CLAUSES. Those clauses may be linked either by a semicolon or by a **coordinating conjunction**, such as "for," "and," "nor," "or," "but," "yet," or "so":

  Huck Finn outsmarts his abusive father; he has to do that in order to survive.

  Odysseus never gives up hope, *and* eventually he triumphs.

- The **complex sentence** contains not only an INDEPENDENT CLAUSE but also one or more **subordinate clauses**. A subordinate clause lacks either a SUBJECT or a PREDICATE and so cannot stand alone as a grammatical unit. A SUBORDINATE CLAUSE may either precede or follow the INDEPENDENT clause in a sentence. In the following examples, the SUBORDINATE clause is in italics:

  When Romeo first sees Juliet, he falls instantly in love with her.

  Elizabeth rejects Mr. Collins's proposal, *which shocks and frustrates him.*

  Although Macbeth acknowledges that murder is evil, he goes through with the assassination of King Duncan.

Means of Linkage: Coordination, Subordination, and Parallelism

The clauses in COMPOUND SENTENCES are linked by what is called **coordination**, meaning the equivalent importance of the two clauses. Writers sometimes intentionally use excessive coordination, especially in successive sentences linked by the neutral "and." One reason is to suggest the childish or simplistic nature of a character's way of speaking or thinking. For example, Daniel Keyes's "Flowers for Algernon" is a science fiction story told in the form of a diary. The NARRATOR is a mentally challenged man who becomes the subject of an operation that increases his intelligence. The following is an entry by the PROTAGONIST before the surgery, describing the aftermath of an intelligence test that the researchers have just given him. The COORDINATING CONJUNCTIONS are italicized.

> I dint get all the words *and* they were talking to fast *but* it sounded like Dr Strauss was on my side *and* like the other one wasn't.
> Then Dr Nemur nodded he said all right maybe your right. We will use Charlie. When he said that I got so exited I jumped up *and* shook his hand for being so good to me. I told him thank you doc you wont be sorry for giving me a second chance. *And* I mean it like I told him.

Charlie's mental limitations are suggested not only by his simple vocabulary and misspelling but also by the excessive coordination that he uses to link clauses and sentences.

Excessive COORDINATION may also be used to create a flat, UNDERSTATED TONE. Here, for example, is the opening paragraph of William Faulkner's SHORT STORY "That Evening Sun." Again, the COORDINATING CONJUNCTIONS are italicized.

> Monday is no different from any other weekday in Jefferson now. The streets are paved now, *and* the telephone and electric companies are cutting down more and more of the shade trees—the water oaks, the maples and locusts and elms—to make room for iron poles bearing clusters of bloated and ghostly and bloodless grapes, *and* we have a city laundry which makes the rounds on Monday morning, gathering the bundles of clothes into bright-colored, specially-made motor cars: the soiled wearing of a whole week now flees apparitionlike behind alert and irritable electric horns, with a long diminishing noise of rubber and asphalt like tearing silk, *and* even the Negro women who still take in white people's washing after the old custom, fetch and deliver it in automobiles.

The long second sentence uses a string of **coordinated clauses** to list the ugly changes that have come to the town. That LOOSE structure suggests the narrator's ironic lack of enthusiasm for the so-called progress.

COMPLEX SENTENCES, in contrast, use a kind of linkage called **subordination**, because it reflects the lesser, or subordinate, importance of the dependent clause. The following passage from Charles

Dickens's *Great Expectations* describes the reaction of the NARRATOR, Pip, to the "desolation" of Miss Havisham, the bitter old woman who raised her ward, Estella, to take revenge upon the entire male sex. Now that her schemes have deprived Pip of the woman he loves, Miss Havisham is remorseful at last. Just before this passage occurs, she has cried, "What have I done!" The **subordinate clauses** are italicized.

> I knew not how to answer, or *how to comfort her. That she had done a grievous thing in taking an impressionable child to mould into the form that her wild resentment, spurned affection, and wounded pride, found vengeance in,* I knew full well. *But that, in shutting out the light of day,* she had shut out infinitely more; *that, in seclusion, she had secluded herself from a thousand natural and healing influences; that her mind, brooding solitary, had grown diseased, as all minds do and must and will that reverse the appointed order of their Maker;* I knew equally well. And could I look upon her without compassion, *seeing her punishment in the ruin she was, in her profound unfitness for this earth on which she was placed, in the vanity of sorrow which had become a master mania, like the vanity of penitence, the vanity of remorse, the vanity of unworthiness, and other monstrous vanities that have been curses in the world*?

The opening COMPLEX SENTENCE contains an INDEPENDENT CLAUSE linked by a COORDINATING CONJUNCTION to a SUBORDINATE CLAUSE that parallels it. The syntax reflects Pip's perplexity about how to react to Miss Havisham's pain. The sentences that follow, all COMPLEX, analyze the aspects of her guilt and of the terrible damage that her vengefulness has done to her own emotional health.

The second sentence begins with a long SUBORDINATE CLAUSE (italicized above) that sums up Miss Havisham's offenses. In a series of PARALLEL PHRASES, it then describes her petty motives. That long list is contrasted with the simple statement of Pip's conviction that he understands her guilt: "I knew full well." The contrast with the elaborate subordinated phrases gives the short INDEPENDENT CLAUSE more force. The next sentence uses several CLAUSES, both SUBORDINATE and INDEPENDENT, to state what Pip knows "equally well": the harm that she has done to herself. The final sentence begins with a simple question, expressing the kindly Pip's compassion even for someone who has ruined his own hopes. He elaborates on that question, "And could I . . . ," in a series of PARALLEL clauses and phrases that build to a ringing climax about the nature of human "vanity."

Another way of signaling the relationships among the parts of a sentence is through **parallelism**. That means making two or more words, phrases, or clauses equivalent in part of speech, grammatical structure, and concept. For instance, in "The Fall of the House of Usher," Edgar Allan Poe modifies the noun "day" with three successive adjectives:

> During the whole of a *dull, dark* and *soundless* day in the autumn of the year . . . I . . . found myself . . . within view of the melancholy House of Usher.

The three parallel adjectives all help to establish the SHORT STORY's SETTING and ATMOSPHERE. In the following example from one of Julius Caesar's speeches, the three INDEPENDENT CLAUSES consist of the same pronoun, followed by a VERB in the past tense:

> I came, I saw, I conquered.

Here, the parallelism serves to build toward a climax: the action expressed in each **parallel clause** is more significant than the last.

Syntactical Order ◀

The **loose** or the **cumulative sentence** presents ideas in the order of subject-verb-object. Sentences written in English typically follow that order. For example, in the following sentence from "A Good Man Is Hard to Find," Flannery O'Connor begins with the main clause (italicized here) and adds modifiers to support it:

> *She pointed out interesting details of the scenery*: Stone Mountain; the blue granite that in some places came up to both sides of the highway; the brilliant red clay banks slightly streaked with purple; and the various crops that made rows of green lace-work on the ground.

Although the elements of the cumulative sentence are connected, they do not have a climactic order, and the sentence would be grammatically complete if it ended earlier. The effect is to create a causal, informal TONE. Here is another example, from Shirley Jackson's SHORT STORY "The Lottery":

> *The rest of the year, the box was put away*, sometimes one place, sometimes another; it had spent one year in Mr. Graves's barn and another year underfoot in the post office, and sometimes it was set on a shelf in the Martin grocery and left there.

The **periodic sentence**, in contrast, is not complete in either syntax or sense until its end. The following example is from Doris Lessing's SHORT STORY "To Room Nineteen":

> It was a long time later that Susan understood that that night, when she had wept and Matthew had driven the misery out of her with his big solid body, was the last time, ever in their married life, that they had been—to use their mutual language—with each other.

By saving its essential phrase, "with each other," for the last and building to a climax, the periodic sentence creates emphasis and suspense. It also tends to sound more formal and declarative than the loose sentence. A famous example is the periodic sentence that opens Franz Kafka's nightmarish tale, "The Metamorphosis":

> As Gregor Samsa awoke one morning from uneasy dreams he found himself transformed in his bed into a gigantic insect.

Writers also sometimes reverse the subject-verb-object order of the usual English sentence to create what is called **inversion**. In the following examples, the inverted word or phrase is italicized, and the standard order is given in brackets:

> *Rarely had* she felt so awkward. [She had rarely felt so awkward.]
>
> *Lying beside the road was* the injured collie. [The injured collie was lying beside the road.]

The technique of inversion is used frequently in poetry, as, for example, in the following COUPLET from Andrew Marvell's "To His Coy Mistress":

> *Had we* but world enough, and time,   [This coyness would not
>   be a crime if we
> This *coyness*, lady, were no crime.   had enough time and
>   worldly life.]

Used in prose, inversion calls attention to the sentence element that is out of typical order and so creates a special kind of emphasis. It also makes the TONE sound more formal and self-conscious. In his inaugural address, for example, President John F. Kennedy employed inversion to memorable effect:

> "*Ask not* [Do not ask . . .]what your country can do for you; ask what you can do for your country."

Sentence Variety ◀

Most writers strive for variety in their use of SYNTAX. For example, striking effects can be created from varying long, COMPLEX SENTENCES with short, SIMPLE ones. The following passage is from Tim O'Brien's fictionalized memoir of his army service in Vietnam, *The Things They Carried*. It describes the lot of the ordinary infantryman (in military jargon the "grunt"), who must carry, literally and METAPHORICALLY, the weight of his duty:

> They carried the land itself—Vietnam, the place, the soil—a powdery orange-red dust that covered their boots and fatigues and faces. They carried the sky. The whole atmosphere, they carried it, the humidity, the monsoons, the stink of fungus and decay, all of it, they carried gravity. They moved like mules. By daylight they took sniper fire, at night they were mortared, but it was not battle, it was just the endless march, village to village, without purpose, nothing won or lost. They marched for the sake of the march. They plodded along slowly, dumbly, leaning forward against the heat, unthinking, all blood and bone, simple grunts, soldiering with their legs, toiling up the hills and down into the paddies and across the rivers and up again and down, just humping, one step and then the next and then another, but no volition, no will, because it was automatic, it was anatomy, and the war was entirely a matter of posture and carriage, the hump was everything, a kind of inertia, a kind of emptiness, a dullness of desire and intellect and conscience and hope and human sensibility. Their principles were in their feet. Their calculations were biological. They had no sense of strategy or mission. They searched the villages without knowing what to look for, not caring, kicking over jars of rice, frisking children and old men, blowing tunnels, sometimes setting fires and sometimes not, then forming up and moving on to the next village, then other villages, where it would always be the same. They carried their own lives. The pressures were enormous.

The NARRATOR suggests the mind-numbing monotony of the march—the "hump"—in the LOOSE COMPOUND SENTENCE that describes the men "plod[ing] along slowly, dumbly." That syntax reflects their step-by-step robotic pace and their "dullness" to all human feeling. In contrast, he uses short, SIMPLE SENTENCES to express their lack of purpose and understanding: "Their principles were in their feet." Once arrived at an arbitrary village, they commit random violence,

▼

described in another long LOOSE SENTENCE. Then they "mov[e] on to the next village," still both dangerous and endangered. To guard against the implication that the men are truly without sense of their situation, the last curt sentence reminds us of the terrible stress they are under.

A style in which too many of the sentences fall into the same syntactical pattern can sound monotonous. At times, however, an author will intentionally repeat a syntactical pattern to create a particular effect, as Tim O'Brien does in the passage above. Another master of that technique is Ernest Hemingway. He was renowned for his use of SIMPLE and COMPOUND SENTENCES to create a TONE of understated tension and fortitude. The following description from his novel *The Sun Also Rises* occurs just after the NARRATOR, Jake Barnes, has had a fistfight with a rival in which he was knocked unconscious:

> Walking across the square to the hotel everything looked new and changed. I had never seen the trees before. I had never seen the flagpoles before, nor the front of the theatre. It was all different. I felt as I felt once coming home from an out-of-town football game. I was carrying a suitcase with my football things in it, and I walked up the street from the station in the town I had lived in all my life and it was all new. They were raking the lawns and burning leaves in the road, and I stopped for a long time and watched. It was all strange. Then I went on, and my feet seemed to be a long way off, and everything seemed to come from a long way off, and I could hear my feet a great distance away. I had been kicked in the head early in the game. It was like that crossing the square. It was like that going up the stairs in the hotel. Going up the stairs took a long time, and I had the feeling that I was carrying my suitcase.

Jake's dazed state of mind is suggested by several means: the short, mostly SIMPLE SENTENCES or COMPOUND SENTENCES linked by neutral "and's," and the repetition of words and phrases (for example, "I had never," "I felt," and "It was like that"). Both light-headed and weighed down by the imaginary suitcase, he seems convincingly the victim of a concussion, an effect created by Hemingway's masterful use of syntax.

Charlotte Brontë, in contrast, wrote in an elaborate style that included LONG COMPLEX SENTENCES, PARALLELISM, and INVERSION. In the following passage from her novel *Jane Eyre*, the ten-year-old PROTAGONIST is describing her adjustment to the rigorous boarding school to which she has been sent. The "grievous load" is a false accusation against her, which has just been disproved.

> Thus relieved of a grievous load, I from that hour set to work afresh, resolved to pioneer my way through every difficulty: I toiled hard, and my success was proportionate to my efforts; my memory, not naturally tenacious, improved with practice: exercise sharpened my wits; in a few weeks I was promoted to a higher class; in less than two months I was allowed to commence French and drawing.

The passage uses SUBORDINATION, INVERSION, COORDINATION, and PARALLELISM to create a long, many-claused sentence. It begins with a SUBORDINATE clause—"Thus relieved of a grievous load." That is followed by an INDEPENDENT clause that INVERTS one of the modifiers: the prepositional phrase "from that hour" precedes, rather than follows, the verb "set to work," calling attention to her determined attitude. A second SUBORDINATE clause further emphasizes that willpower: "resolved to pioneer my way through every difficulty."

Instead of ending the sentence there, the NARRATOR links it with a colon to the results of her resolution. The first result is a generalization about her approach expressed in two INDEPENDENT CLAUSES, linked with the COORDINATING CONJUNCTION "and": "I toiled hard, and my success was proportionate to my efforts." The sentence then continues with a series of PARALLEL clauses. The first two describe the means to her success: "my memory, not naturally tenacious, improved with practice" and "exercise sharpened my wits." Two last PARALLEL clauses specify the time that passes and the rewards that result: "in a few weeks I was promoted to a higher class; in less than two months I was allowed to commence French and drawing."

The effect of this long, balanced sentence is to convey a sense of the determination with which the narrator applies herself and the steady pace at which she achieves success. The SYNTAX reflects the content. It suggests through the precise, step-by-step structure that effect is clearly linked to cause, and that hard effort will lead to progress.

As the examples above suggest, a writer's choices about syntax have important effects on the meaning and TONE of a work. They are also key to establishing his or her individual style. See also DICTION.

EXERCISES: Syntax

I. For each of the following passages:

- Identify the kind(s) of sentence that it contains: SIMPLE, COMPOUND, or COMPLEX.
- State whether each is LOOSE or PERIODIC, and explain the basis for that choice.
- If the passage contains an intentional SENTENCE FRAGMENT, explain its effect.

1. I am getting angry enough to do something desperate. To jump out of the window would be admirable exercise, but the bars are too strong even to try.

    Besides I wouldn't do it. Of course not.

    —CHARLOTTE PERKINS GILMAN, "The Yellow Wall-paper"

2. It is a truth universally acknowledged, that a single man in possession of a good fortune, must be in want of a wife.

    —JANE AUSTEN, *Pride and Prejudice*

3. After a night behind the scenes, Paul found the schoolroom more than ever repulsive; the bare floors and naked walls; the prosy men who never wore frock coats, or violets in their buttonholes; the women with their dull gowns, shrill voices, and pitiful seriousness about prepositions that govern the dative.

    —WILLA CATHER, "Paul's Case"

4. Knowing that Mrs. Mallard was afflicted with a heart trouble, great care was taken to break to her as gently as possible the news of her husband's death.　　—KATE CHOPIN, "The Story of an Hour"

II. For each of the following passages, specify the means of linkage that it exemplifies—COORDINATION, SUBORDINATION, PARALLELISM, or INVERSION—and explain the basis for that choice. Note that some examples may use more than one kind of linkage.

1. While of other law-copyists I might write the complete life, of Bartleby nothing of the sort can be done.

    —HERMAN MELVILLE, "Bartleby the Scrivener"

2. It is to be observed, that these ambassadors spoke to me by an interpreter; the languages of both empires differing as much from each other as any two in Europe, and each nation priding itself upon the antiquity, beauty, and energy of their own tongues, with an avowed contempt for that of their neighbor; yet our Emperor, standing upon the advantage he had got by the seizure of their fleet, obliged them to deliver their credentials, and make their speech, in the Lilliputian tongue.

–JONATHAN SWIFT, *Gulliver's Travels*

3. *After speculating that a woman who had tried to become a playwright in Shakespeare's day would have been under enormous stress, Virginia Woolf continues:*

And undoubtedly, I thought, looking at the shelf where there are no plays by women, her work would have gone unsigned. That refuge she would have sought certainly.

–VIRGINIA WOOLF, *A Room of One's Own*

4. But the thing did not then leave the vicinity of the boat. Ahead or astern, on one side or the other, at intervals long or short, fled the long sparkling streak, and there was to be heard the *whirroo* of the dark fin. –STEPHEN CRANE, "The Open Boat"

Prosody

Prosody is a term that describes the technical aspects of verse relating to rhythm, stress, and meter.

METER

Meter is the recurring pattern of sounds that gives poems written in VERSE their distinctive rhythms. (Many POEMS, especially those written since the nineteenth century, do not use regular meter or consistent RHYME. The term for that open form is FREE VERSE.) The recurrence of rhythms is basic to human life. It is tied to our breathing, our heartbeats, and such natural cycles as the ebb and flow of the tides and the processes of birth and death. In fact, the random rhythms of ordinary speech may sometimes fall into meter. The distinguishing feature of poetic meter, however, is that such rhythms recur in sustained and regular patterns. Meter, like other aspects of sound in POETRY, is a crucial aspect of meaning. The system for marking meter and analyzing its effects, called SCANSION, will be described at the end of this section.

The most common metrical system in English verse, from the fourteenth century on, is **accentual-syllabic meter.** As the name indicates, it is based both on the number of syllables in a line and on the pattern of stresses in each metrical unit, or **foot.**

Several factors determine where the stresses fall in a line of verse. The first is the normal pattern of stresses in the pronunciation of individual words and phrases, for example: óthĕr, prŏvíde, dángĕrŏus, ŏn thĕ tóp, ĭndĭvídŭăl. The unstressed syllable is indicated by a crescent, the stressed by an acute accent. Another factor is the relative importance of the words in the line. For example, in the sentence "Look at me," either the first or the last word could be stressed, depending on how the speaker wanted to direct the listener's attention: "Lóok at me" or "Look at mé." Finally, the words' grammatical functions influence their stress. For example, nouns, verbs, and adjectives, the major parts of speech, tend to be accented more strongly to show their importance, while articles and prepositions are usually stressed lightly.

We naturally "hear" such stresses as we read and listen, especially when they recur, as they do in lines of poetry. Readers must be taught, however, the terms for various metrical units and the system for recording them. That process is comparable to learning to read music. For example, the following lines of William Blake's "Song" have clear and regular metrical feet:

Hŏw swéet / Ĭ roám'd / frŏm fiéld / tŏ fiéld
Ănd tást / ĕd áll / thĕ súm / mĕr's príde.

A foot may contain more than a single word. Also, a word may be divided between different feet, as with "tasted" and "summer" above. In marking a line of verse, a slash is used to separate the individual feet.

METRICAL FEET

Iambic (eye-AM-bick; the noun is iamb: EYE-amb), an unstressed followed by a stressed syllable:

Hĕ thoúght / hĕ képt / thĕ ú / nĭvérse / ălóne.

—ROBERT FROST, "The Most of It"

The example from Blake's "Song" is also iambic. The iamb has been said to imitate the soft/loud sound of a heartbeat.

Anapestic (an-uh-PES-tick; the noun is anapest: AN-uh-pest), two unstressed syllables followed by a stressed one; for example:

Ănd thĕ eýes / ŏf thĕ sléep / ĕrs wăxed déad / lў ănd chíll,
Ănd thĕir heárts / bŭt ŏnce heáved, / ănd fŏré / vĕr grĕw stíll!

—GEORGE GORDON, LORD BYRON, "The Destruction of Sennacherib"

Trochaic (troh-KAY-ick; the noun is trochee: TROH-key), a stressed syllable followed by an unstressed syllable:

Dóu blĕ, / dóublĕ, / tóil ănd / tróublĕ,
Fíre / búrn ănd / caúldrŏn / búbblĕ.

—WILLIAM SHAKESPEARE, Macbeth

Dactylic (dak-TILL-ic, or the dactyl: DAK-till), a stressed syllable followed by two that are unstressed:

Cánnŏn ĭn / frónt ŏf thĕm
Vóllĕyed ănd / thúndĕred.

—ALFRED, LORD TENNYSON, "The Charge of the Light Brigade"

Here, the first line and the first foot of the second line are regular dactyls; the last foot lacks the final unstressed syllable.

Number of Feet in a Line

In describing a poem's meter, one needs to name the metrical foot and to specify the number of feet in each line. This number is indicated by terms derived from Greek. The most common are the following:

Monometer (mon-OM-eh-ter), one foot. Such a line usually occurs only as a variant in poems comprised largely of longer lines. In the following example, only the third and fourth lines are **monometric**:

> Though she / were true / when you / met her,
> And last / till you / write your / letter,
>> Yet she
>> Will be
> False, ere / I come, / to two, / or three.

—JOHN DONNE, "Song"

Dimeter (DIM-eh-ter), two feet:

> Wild nights— / Wild nights!
> Were I / with thee
> Wild nights / should be
> Our lux / ury!

—EMILY DICKINSON, "Wild nights"

Trimeter (TRIM-eh-ter), three feet:

> We romped / until / the pans
> Slid from / the kit / chen shelf;
> My mo / ther's coun / tenance
> Could not / unfrown / itself.

—THEODORE ROETHKE, "My Papa's Waltz"

Tetrameter (te-TRAM-eh-ter), four feet:

> She walks / in beau / ty, like / the night
>> Of cloud / less climes / and star / ry skies.

—GEORGE GORDON, Lord Byron, "She Walks in Beauty"

Pentameter (pen-TAM-eh-ter), five feet:

> When I / have fears / that I / may cease / to be
>> Before / my pen / has gleaned / my teem / ing brain.

—JOHN KEATS, "When I Have Fears"

Naming the Meter ◀

The meter is designated by combining the adjectival name for the foot with the term that specifies the number of feet in a line. For example, a line comprised of five iambs would be labeled **iambic pentameter**:

> When you / are old / and grey / and full / of sleep,
> And nod / ding by / the fire, / take down / this book.
> —WILLIAM BUTLER YEATS, "When You Are Old"

Iambic pentameter is the meter closest to the rhythm of ordinary English speech. To take a prose example: "I think / that you / can hear / this rhy / thm now." For that reason, it is the most common meter in English poetry of every age. See also BLANK VERSE.

To cite a few more examples of names for meter, the following lines, made up of three feet of trochees, are in **trochaic trimeter**:

> Higher / still and / higher
>   From the / earth thou / springest
> Like a / cloud of / fire
>   The deep / blue thou / wingest
> —PERCY BYSSHE SHELLEY, "To a Skylark"

This line, comprised of four dactyls, is in **dactylic tetrameter**:

> Woman much / missed, how you / call to me, / call to me
> —THOMAS HARDY, "The Voice"

An important consideration is that few poems fall into a regular, unvarying meter. In fact, rigidly regular meter tends to be monotonous and simplistic. It is often the variations in a poem's basic meter that give a line special power.

Common Substitutions ◀

Any variant foot within a line that consists predominantly of another metrical pattern is called a **substitution**. The most common substitutions are the following:

A **spondaic** (spahn-DAY-ick) **foot**, or **spondee** (SPAHN-dee), two stressed syllables in a row:

> Roúgh wińds / dó sháke / the dar / ling buds / of May,
> And sum / mer's lease / hath all / tóo shórt / a date.
> —WILLIAM SHAKESPEARE, Sonnet 18

Here, the first foot of the iambic pentameter first line and the fourth foot of the next are spondees. The second foot in the first line ("do shake") might also be considered a spondee, as it is here. Some readers, though, might hear it as a regular IAMB, in keeping with the rest of the line: "dŏ sháke." There is room for such variation in marking individual feet; expert readers would not disagree, however, on the predominant METER or on the strong spondees cited.

A TROCHEE at the start of an IAMBIC line:

> Géttĭng / and spend / ing, we / lay waste / our powers;
> Líttlĕ / we see / in Na / ture that / is ours.
> > —WILLIAM WORDSWORTH, "The World Is Too Much with Us"

Lines that end with a strong stress, such as the examples of trimeter and tetrameter on p. 120, are said to have a **masculine ending**. The following is a regular IAMBIC PENTAMETER line with a masculine ending:

> Ĭ wáke / tŏ sléep / ănd táke / mў wák / ĭng slów.
> > —THEODORE ROETHKE, "The Waking"

Lines that end in an unstressed syllable, as do regular TROCHAIC and DACTYLIC lines, such as those on p. 121, are said to have a **feminine ending**.

Another common SUBSTITUTION is an added unstressed syllable at the end of an IAMBIC line:

> Tŏ bé / ŏr nót / tŏ bé, / thát ĭs / thĕ qués / tiŏn.
> > —WILLIAM SHAKESPEARE, *Hamlet*

> Thĕ whís / kĕy ón / yŏur bréath
> Cŏuld máke / ă smáll / bŏy díz /zў.
> > —THEODORE ROETHKE, "My Papa's Waltz"

Often, as in these cases, the final unstressed syllable can be a subtle sign that the speaker is off balance or uncertain.

Pauses Within and Between Lines of Verse

The other key indication of poetic rhythm is in the pauses that occur, both between and within lines of verse:

End-stopped lines contain a complete sentence or independent clause and so have a distinct pause at the end, usually indicated by a mark of punctuation:

The sea is calm tonight.

—MATTHEW ARNOLD, "Dover Beach"

Little Lamb, who made thee?
Dost thou know who made thee?

—WILLIAM BLAKE, "The Lamb"

End-stopped lines call attention to the complete thought expressed in the single line.

Enjambed lines (en-JAMMED; the noun is **enjambment**), also called **run-on lines**, are those in which the sentence or clause continues for two or more lines of verse. No punctuation appears at the end of the enjambed lines:

She is as in a field a silken tent
At midday when a sunny summer breeze
Has dried the dew and all its ropes relent,

—ROBERT FROST, "The Silken Tent"

The first two lines are enjambed, the third end-stopped. Here the effect of the enjambment is to give a more leisurely pace to the lines. The luxurious billowing of the "silken tent," and therefore the attractiveness of the woman being compared to it, is suggested by the clause stretching out over three lines.

Another effect can be to call attention to the words that appear at the end and the beginning of the enjambed lines:

The glamour

Of childish days is upon me, my manhood is cast
Down in the flood of remembrance, I weep like a child for the
    past.

—D. H. LAWRENCE, "Piano"

Here, the enjambment gives special emphasis to "cast" and "down," so that the narrator's giving way to helpless weeping is reflected in the structure of the lines.

A **caesura** (say-ZYOOR-a) is a pause in the midst of a verse line. The pause is indicated by a mark of punctuation, such as a comma, a question mark, a period, or a dash. The effect of a caesura is to create a shift in the rhythmic pattern of a line, which parallels a shift in its focus. In scanning a poem, **caesuras** are marked with a double slash:

St. Agnes' Eve—// Ah, // bitter chill it was!
The owl, // for all his feathers, // was a-cold.

—JOHN KEATS, "The Eve of St. Agnes"

▼

Scansion

The process of analyzing and marking the type and the number of feet in each line of verse is called **scansion**. A reader **scans** several lines to determine the basic metrical foot that the poet is using. Then he or she counts the number of feet that a typical line or, in some poems, a varying pattern of lines contain. (For example, in **ballad meter**, IAMBIC TETRAMETER alternates with IAMBIC TRIMETER.) It is important to note that scansion is not an exact art. Ambiguities exist about the degrees of stress and the meter of some lines. Expert readers would agree, however, on the predominant meter of a poem.

Poets tend to choose a given meter and its variations not for mechanical reasons but, rather like verbal musicians, they use this aspect of sound to create TONE and express certain meanings. The effects of meter are often subtle. Highly regular meter can signal a positive TONE, a narrator who feels in tune with the world and content, as in Christina Rossetti's "Up-Hill." In contrast, a highly irregular meter can imply distress or uncertainty, as in Byron's "When We Two Parted." This distinction is not absolute, however. Regular meter can be used to convey an outraged tone, as in William Blake's "London." Regular meter can also be used for ironic contrast. For example, a poem's surface may be rhythmic and melodic but its underlying meaning may be pessimistic or eerie, as in Emily Dickinson's "Because I could not stop for Death."

In some poems, the tone undergoes an important shift, especially near the end. Two examples are the eventual tranquility and acceptance of George Herbert's rebellious speaker in "The Collar," and the final desperation of Blake's initially carefree lover in "How Sweet I Roam'd from Field to Field." SUBSTITUTIONS tend to occur most often at the start of poems and in the first lines of a stanza. The surest way to determine the predominant meter is to scan some lines in the middle of the poem. Once both the prevalent pattern and the variations in it have been noted, the reader can be more alert to the effects of such choices on the poem's TONE and meaning.

EXERCISES: Meter

I. Scan the meter of the following passages of poetry.

- Mark the STRESSED and UNSTRESSED SYLLABLES.
- Separate the FEET with slashes.
- Name the METER. *Note:* Some examples may contain more than one kind of METER.

1. A Chapel was built in the midst,
   Where I used to play on the green.

   —WILLIAM BLAKE, "The Garden of Love"

2. The woods decay, the woods decay and fall,
   The vapors weep their burthen to the ground,
   Man comes and tills the field and lies beneath,
   And after many a summer dies the swan.

   —ALFRED, LORD TENNYSON, "Tithonus"

3. Earth, receive an honoured guest:
   William Yeats is laid to rest.
   Let the Irish vessel lie
   Emptied of its poetry.

   —W. H. AUDEN, "In Memory of W. B. Yeats"

II. Substitutions. For each of the following passages:

- Scan the lines, marking the STRESSED and UNSTRESSED SYLLABLES and separating the FEET with slashes.
- Name the predominant METER.
- List any SUBSTITUTIONS that occur. *Note:* Some examples may contain more than one.
- Describe the effects of the SUBSTITUTIONS on the TONE and meaning.

1. Ah! well-a-day! what evil looks
   Had I from old and young!
   Instead of the cross, the Albatross
   About my neck was hung.

   —SAMUEL TAYLOR COLERIDGE, "The Rime of the Ancient Mariner"

2. The hand that held my wrist
   Was battered on one knuckle;
   At every step you missed
   My right ear scraped a buckle.

   —THEODORE ROETHKE, "My Papa's Waltz"

3. The dew of the morning
      Sunk chill on my brow—
   It felt like the warning
      Of what I feel now.

   —GEORGE GORDON, LORD BYRON, "When We Two Parted"

III. Pauses. For each of the following passages:

- Say whether each line is END-STOPPED or ENJAMBED.
- Mark any CAESURAS.
- Explain the effects of those choices on the TONE and meaning.

1. How do I love thee? Let me count the ways.
    I love thee to the depth and breadth and height
    My soul can reach, when feeling out of sight
    For the ends of being and ideal grace.
    —ELIZABETH BARRETT BROWNING, from *Sonnets from the Portuguese* (43)

2. I wandered lonely as a cloud
    That floats on high o'er vales and hills,
    When all at once I saw a crowd,
    A host, of golden daffodils.
    —WILLIAM WORDSWORTH, "I Wandered Lonely as a Cloud"

3. No longer mourn for me when I am dead
    Than you shall hear the surly sullen bell
    Give warning to the world that I am fled
    From this vile world, with vilest worms to dwell.
    —WILLIAM SHAKESPEARE, Sonnet 71

RHYME

Rhyme is the repetition in two or more nearby words of the last stressed vowel and all the syllables that follow it. Rhyme does not have to be an element of poetry, as the many works written in BLANK VERSE and FREE VERSE prove. Poetry is the LITERARY FORM, however, that uses rhyme systematically and extensively. Something about rhyme is pleasing to the human ear, as is clear from the delight with which small children respond to nursery rhymes. It recalls poetry's earliest origins in song and, like METER, can be an important element in a work's verbal music.

This is not to suggest, however, that rhyme need be merely decorative. It can serve several important functions. Perhaps most important, rhyme may be used to create unity, by setting up and confirming a pattern in which sound and meaning concur. It can link or contrast ideas and put STRESS on particular words.

Rhyme may also signal a surprising departure if it does not occur in the expected place. Shakespeare includes rhymed passages in the BLANK VERSE form of his plays for variety and emphasis, as do modern poets writing in FREE VERSE.

End Rhyme

Most rhymes occur at the end of the poetic line. The term for this is
end rhyme. The rhyme may consist of only one syllable, as in "fónd"
and "pónd," or it may be multisyllabic: "hásty / tásty." If two of the
syllables rhyme, as in the second example, the rhyme is called **double**. Rhymes that end on a STRESSED syllable, such as "fond / pond"
and "on the spot / in the pot," are called **masculine**. Rhymes that
end on an UNSTRESSED syllable, as do "hasty / tasty" and "attention /
dimension," are called **feminine**. See also POETIC FORMS.

Internal Rhyme

Rhymes may also occur within a line of poetry rather than at the
end, as in this example from William Blake's "The Garden of Love":

And binding with *briars* my joys & *desires*.

In this case, the device is called **internal rhyme**. Edgar Allan Poe
used that technique extensively in "The Raven":

Ah, distinctly I *remember* it was in the bleak *December*,
And each separate dying *ember* wrought its ghost upon the floor.
Eagerly I wished the *morrow*;—vainly I had sought to *borrow*
From my books surcease of *sorrow*—sorrow for the lost
    Lenore—
For the rare and radiant maiden whom the angels name
    Lenore—
                                    Nameless here for evermore.

Here, the combination of internal rhymes and repetitive END RHYMES
helps create the poem's chantlike tone and claustrophobic atmosphere.

Rhyme Scheme

When a poem is SCANNED, rhymes are marked with letters of the alphabet, with the first rhyme designated as *a*, the second as *b*, etc. The
pattern of recurrences is called a **rhyme scheme**. For example, the following stanza from William Wordsworth's "Three Years She Grew" has
a rhyme scheme of *aabccb*. No letters are used to mark INTERNAL RHYME.

Three years she grew in sun and shower   *a*
Then Nature said, "A lovelier flower   *a*

> On earth was never sown;   *b*
> This Child I to myself will take;   *c*
> She shall be mine, and I will make   *c*
> A Lady of my own."   *b*

Unlike this example, some stanzaic patterns are identified by particular rhyme schemes, for example, the SONNET, the COUPLET, and BALLAD METER.

In "Dover Beach," Matthew Arnold uses a highly irregular RHYME SCHEME to moving effect. To take a sample STANZA:

> The Sea of Faith   *a*
> Was once, too, at the full, and round earth's shore   *b*
> Lay like the folds of a bright girdle furled.   *c*
> But now I only hear   *d*
> Its melancholy, long withdrawing roar,   *b*
> Retreating, to the breath   *a*
> Of the night-wind, down the vast edges drear   *d*
> And naked shingles[1] of the world.   *c*

The lack of recurrent pattern in either the rhyme or the METER reflects the breakdown of order that the narrator laments and foreshadows the oncoming chaos.

Perfect and Imperfect Rhyme

When the rhyming sounds match exactly, as in the Wordsworth poem above, the rhyme is called **perfect**. An alternative form is **eye rhyme**, in which words look on the page like perfect rhymes but over time have come to be pronounced differently: "cover / over," "bough / tough."

Rhymes may also be partial rather than perfect. In that case, the corresponding vowel sounds and/or the consonant sounds vary, as in the following pairs from Emily Dickinson's "A Bird Came Down the Walk": "abroad / head," "Crumb / Home," and "seam / swim." That device is called by a variety of terms: **imperfect rhyme**, **half rhyme**, **off-rhyme**, and **slant rhyme**. Because imperfect rhyme does not fulfill the expectation of exactly chiming syllables that perfect rhyme would lead us to anticipate, it can create a disconcerting effect. Wilfred Owen's "Insensibility," a denouncement of those who are indifferent

---

1. Beaches covered with small stones.

to the suffering caused by war, makes ingenious use of half rhyme. It includes such paired words as "killed / cold," "fooling / filling," and "red / rid." The final stanza contains a stinging condemnation:

> But cursed are dullards whom no cannon stuns,
> That they should be as stones.
> Wretched are they, and mean
> With paucity that never was simplicity.
> By choice they made themselves immune
> To pity and whatever moans in man.

The half rhyme of "stuns / stones" underlines the narrator's scorn of such "dullards." The linking of "mean / immune / moan / man" implies the contrast between pettiness and indifference and the empathy for others' pain that is the essence of humane feeling. In SCANSION, eye rhymes and half rhymes are marked in the same way as perfect rhymes, with sequential letters of the alphabet.

Half rhyme has been used as a minor device in English poetry from the earliest times, particularly in folk ballads. Since the mid-nineteenth century, it has been a prominent feature in the work of several poets. In addition to Dickinson and Owen, other innovative users of half rhyme have included William Butler Yeats, W. H. Auden, Adrienne Rich, and Seamus Heaney. Often, poets vary perfect with imperfect rhyme.

EXERCISE: Rhyme

For each of the following passages:

- Mark the RHYME SCHEME, both with letters of the alphabet at the ends of lines and with the rhyme pattern of the stanza—e.g., abab.
- Name the kind(s) of rhyme that the passage uses: PERFECT RHYME, HALF RHYME, or EYE RHYME.
- Mark any INTERNAL RHYMES by underlining the rhyming words.
- Specify whether each rhyme is MASCULINE or FEMININE.
- Describe the effects of the rhyme on the TONE and meaning of the passage.
  Note: Some passages may contain more than one kind of rhyme; in those cases, identify each kind and describe its effects.

1. I wander thro' each charter'd[1] street
    Near where the charter'd Thames does flow,

---

1. Mapped; rented out.

▼

And mark in every face I meet
Marks of weakness, marks of woe.

— WILLIAM BLAKE, "London"

2. If this be error and upon me proved,
   I never writ, nor no man ever loved.

— WILLIAM SHAKESPEARE, Sonnet 116

3. "Hope" is the thing with feathers—
   That perches in the soul—
   And sings the song without the words—
   And never stops—at all—

— EMILY DICKINSON, "'Hope' is the thing with feathers"

4. The splendor falls on castle walls
       And snowy summits old in story:
   The long light shakes across the lakes,
       And the wild cataract² leaps in glory.
   Blow, bugle, blow, set the wild echoes flying,   5
   Blow, bugle; answer, echoes, dying, dying, dying.

— ALFRED, LORD TENNYSON, "The Splendor Falls"

5. Nobody heard him, the dead man,
   But still he lay moaning:
   I was much further out than you thought
   And not waving but drowning.

— STEVIE SMITH, "Not Waving but Drowning"

6. Gather ye rosebuds while ye may,
       Old time is still a-flying;
   And this same flower that smiles today
       Tomorrow will be dying.
   The glorious lamp of heaven, the sun,   5
       The higher he's a getting,
   The sooner will his race be run,
       And nearer he's to setting.

— ROBERT HERRICK, "To the Virgins, to Make Much of Time"

---

2. Waterfall.

SOUND AND SOUND PATTERNS

In addition to RHYME, several other recurrent patterns of sound may be used to create unity and emphasis.

Alliteration

Alliteration, the repetition of sounds in nearby words or stressed syllables, is frequent in both poetry and prose. Usually, the term applies to consonants that appear at the beginnings of words. For example, in Gwendolyn Brooks's "We Real Cool," the young delinquents who serve as the group of NARRATORS boast of their dangerous lifestyle: "We / Lurk late. We / Strike straight." The alliterated *l* and *s* sounds link the curt statements. The alliteration suggests the speakers' bravado and their eagerness to promote their "cool" and threatening image. As with all patterns of sound, including RHYME, such effects depend on the combination of repeated sounds and of the meanings of the words in which the sounds occur.

Another effect of alliteration may be comic exaggeration. The title of Jane Austen's novel *Pride and Prejudice* uses alliteration to imply the connection between the faults of character that the book will satirize. Shakespeare called attention to the comic effect of excessive alliteration in *A Midsummer Night's Dream*. In the final act, a group of dull-witted Athenian laborers stage a performance of a DOGGEREL tragedy. Their crude production, Shakespeare's parody of Elizabethan theater, contains such silly passages as the following APOSTROPHE. The hero, believing that his love, whom he calls his "dainty duck," is dead, calls for the Fates to strike him, too:

> O Fates, come, come,
> Cut thread and thrum,[1]
> Quail,[2] crush, conclude, and quell[3]!

The humor lies in the excessiveness of the alliteration and the redundancy of the synonyms that it links. As this passage shows, alliteration depends on the way that words sound, not on their spelling: here, "cut" and "quail" alliterate. To take a second example, "gnaw," "know," and "new" alliterate, but "gnaw" and "get" do not. The repeated sound may also occur within words, as in "conclude" above; in that case, it is called **internal alliteration**.

---

1. Weaving: loose end of thread.
2. Overpower.
3. Kill.

    Used for serious purposes, alliteration may subtly create unity and influence TONE. In Walt Whitman's "A Noiseless, Patient Spider," the narrator describes the creature beginning to construct its web: "It launched *forth filament, filament, filament*, out of itself." The alliterated *f* suggests the step-by-step nature of the process, as well as the spider's determination. In William Butler Yeats's "The Lake Isle of Innisfree," the narrator uses alliteration to describe a beloved place: "I hear *lake* water *lapping* with *low* sounds by the shore." The repeated *l*, which linguists call a "liquid" sound, suggests the tranquil atmosphere of the idyllic setting.

    In Shakespeare's *Macbeth*, the PROTAGONIST reflects in an early SOLILOQUY on his qualms about murdering kind old King Duncan, who stands in the way of Macbeth's ambition for the throne of Scotland:

> If th'assassination
> Could trammel up[4] the *consequence* and *catch*
> With his *surcease*[5] *success*[6]—that *but* this *blow*
> Might *be* the *be*-all and the end-all!—here,
> But here, upon this *bank* and shoal[7] of time,
> We'd *jump* the life to *come*.

Lines 2–4 are full of alliterated *s* sounds, initial and internal. They underline the secrecy and egotism of Macbeth's impossible hope: that the "assassination" could be done in a self-contained moment of time and produce no further "consequence." The hissing *s* sound betrays his recognition of his evil purpose, however. That effect is enhanced by the repeated *b*'s that suggest the "blows" he plans to deal his innocent victim.

Assonance

Assonance (ASS-oh-nantz) is the repetition of identical or similar vowel sounds in nearby words or stressed syllables: "*right* / *time*," "*sad* / *fact*," "*seven* / *elves*." It differs from RHYME, in which both the vowels and the consonants of nearby words match. As the examples above show, the **assonantal** sound may occur either at the beginning

---

4. Trap in a net.
5. Duncan's death.
6. Victory; also, something that occurs afterwards.
7. Riverbank and shallows.

of words or in the middle. Like ALLITERATION, it can create underlying harmony as well as provide coherence and emphasis.

In the opening lines of John Keats's "Ode on a Grecian Urn," the narrator uses assonance in APOSTROPHIZING the work of art:

> Thou still unravished bride of quietness,
>   Thou foster child of silence and slow time.

The repetition of the short *i* sound in "still unravished" emphasizes the meaning of those words. It also suggests the speaker's first impression of wonder at the ancient urn's pure state. The long *i* that predominates suggests the serenity and self-possession of the urn. Despite the metaphors of human relationship—the urn is compared to a "bride" and a "foster child"—the implication is that art is unmoved by human passions.

Assonance conveys a very different tone in Tennyson's *In Memoriam*. The narrator, grieving over the death of a beloved friend, recalls waiting eagerly to take his hand. Then he laments:

> A hand that can be clasped no more—
>   Behold me, for I cannot sleep.

The repeated short *a* sounds, reinforced by the ALLITERATED *c*'s, like quick blows, imply the cruelty and permanance of the loss. The long *e*'s suggest the reaction: a near wail of despair.

Onomatopoeia ◀

Onomatopoeia (ah-noh-maht-oh-PEE-ah) means using a word or phrase that seems to imitate the sound it denotes: for example, "bang," "creak," "murmur," "ding-dong," or "plop." As with ALLITERATION and ASSONANCE, that effect cannot come from the sound of the word alone: its meaning is involved as well. To illustrate, words whose sounds closely resemble those of some of the examples above—"bank," "creek," and "plot"—are not **onomatopoeic**.

In "Piano," D. H. Lawrence uses onomatopoeia to echo the sounds that a small child hears as he sits under the piano while his mother plays, "in the *boom* of the *tingling* strings." The description implies that, with his ear so close to the sound box, the boy hears both the "boom" of the music and the "tingling strings" of the keys that the musician presses to create it. Lewis Carroll makes clever use of onomatopoeia in "Jabberwocky," a nonsense poem about a boy who slays a dragon-like monster. Carroll's invention of "portmanteau" words, created by combining two standard words, includes some that are onomatopoeic. For example, as the Jabberwock goes on the attack, it "burble[s]," a word that seems to be made up of "bubble" and "burp." Few young readers would likely be frightened by a creature that makes such a silly noise, or by the "snicker-snack" that describes the Jabberwock's quick and bloodless beheading. The light tone is sustained by the reaction of the boy's father, who "chortle[s]" (probably a combination of "chuckle" and "snort") his joyful congratulations.

As these examples show, the various sound patterns may coexist with one another, for example, ONOMATOPOEIA with ASSONANCE ("in the boom of the tingling strings") in the line above from "Piano" by Lawrence. Also, it should be stressed again that none of these patterns depend solely on the sound of words: rather, their richness and force derive from the associations that they present between sound and meaning.

EXERCISES: Sound and Sound Patterns

For each of the following passages:
- Name the predominant SOUND PATTERN: ALLITERATION, ASSONANCE, or ONOMATOPOEIA.
- Underline the letters or words that display that SOUND PATTERN.
- Describe the effects of the SOUND PATTERN(s) on the meaning and the TONE of the passage.
  Note: Some passages may contain more than one sound pattern; in those cases, identify each kind and describe its effects.

1. He clasps the crag with crooked hands,
   Close to the sun in lonely lands.
   —ALFRED, LORD TENNYSON, "The Eagle"

2. A tap at the pane, the quick sharp scratch
   And blue spurt of a lighted match . . .
   —ROBERT BROWNING, "Meeting at Night"

3. In me thou see'st the twilight of such day
   As after sunset fadeth in the west;
   Which by and by black night doth take away,
   Death's second self, that seals up all in rest.
   —WILLIAM SHAKESPEARE, Sonnet 73

4. The hum of multitudes was there, but multitudes of lambs,
   Thousands of little boys & girls raising their innocent hands.
   —WILLIAM BLAKE, "Holy Thursday [I]"

5. And the silken, sad, uncertain rustling of each purple curtain
   Thrilled me—filled me with fantastic terrors never felt before.
   —EDGAR ALLAN POE, "The Raven"

Poetic Forms

The term **poetic form** indicates the way that a poem is structured by recurrent patterns of rhythms and words. In English poetry, there are three main types of structure: (1) STANZAS, which have a recurrent pattern of METER, line length, and RHYME; (2) BLANK VERSE, which has a recurrent pattern of METER and line length but without RHYME; and (3) FREE VERSE, which lacks both recurrent METER and RHYME but is structured by a variety of rhythmic and verbal patterns.

The REFRAIN is a word, phrase, line, or group of lines that is repeated at intervals. While not a separate poetic form, it is a feature of some poetic STANZAS. Other forms describe the structure of an entire poem. Only the most widely used, the SONNET, is dealt with in this book.

STANZAS

A **stanza** is a group of lines in a poem that share a common pattern of METER, line length, and RHYME. Some of the most common types of **stanzas** are discussed below.

Couplet

A **couplet** is a pair of rhymed lines of the same length and METER. This example, from Ben Jonson's short lyric "Still to Be Neat," is an IAMBIC TETRAMETER couplet:

> Give me a look, give me a face
> That makes simplicity a grace.

Rhymed pairs of lines in IAMBIC PENTAMETER (five feet of alternating unstressed and stressed syllables) are termed **heroic couplets**. That term recalls their frequent use in epics and heroic plays, genres that depict the deeds of heroes.

The **closed couplet** is a pair of lines in which the end of the rhyme coincides with the end of the clause or sentence, as shown in Alexander Pope's "The Rape of the Lock":

> Bright as the sun, her eyes the gazers strike,
> And, like the sun, they shine on all alike.

In order to maintain the closed form, poets use END-STOPPED lines, CAESURAS, and MASCULINE line endings to put emphasis on the rhyming words.

In contrast, **open couplets** are fluent. The rhyme is not insistent, but it subtly underlies the METER. One example is Robert Browning's DRAMATIC MONOLOGUE "My Last Duchess":

>   Sir, 'twas not
> Her husband's presence only called that spot
> Of joy into the Duchess' cheek: perhaps
> Frà Pandolf chanced to say "Her mantle laps
> Over my lady's wrist too much," or "Paint   5
> Must never hope to reproduce the faint
> Half-flush that dies along her throat": such stuff
> Was courtesy, she thought, and cause enough
> For calling up that spot of joy.

Here, the ENJAMBMENTS (the lengthy phrases and sentences, which run over the ends of the poetic lines) give the poem a casual, conversational TONE. It comes as a surprise to realize that the monologue is written in couplets rather than in BLANK VERSE.

Quatrain   ◄

The **quatrain**, consisting of four lines, is the most common STANZA form in English poetry. A quatrain may use a variety of METERS and RHYME SCHEMES. The most frequent RHYME SCHEME is that in which the second and fourth lines rhyme (*abcb*). One example is William Blake's "The Garden of Love," in which the predominant meter is ANAPESTIC TRIMETER:

> I went to the Garden of Love,
> And saw what I never had seen:
> A Chapel was built in the midst,
> Where I used to play on the green.

The OCTAVE of the ITALIAN SONNET consists of two quatrains, and the SHAKESPEAREAN SONNET contains three quatrains and a COUPLET.

One of the most commonly used quatrains in English poetry is **ballad meter**, alternating IAMBIC TETRAMETER and IAMBIC TRIMETER. Typically the second and fourth lines rhyme. An example is Samuel Taylor Coleridge's "The Rime of the Ancient Mariner":

> All in a hot and copper sky,
> The bloody Sun, at noon,
> Right up above the mast did stand,
> No bigger than the moon.

The term derives from the stanza's frequent use in folk songs, such as the anonymous "Sir Patrick Spens."

Ballad meter was a favorite with Emily Dickinson, who used it with striking imagination and variety:

> I felt a Funeral, in my Brain,
> And Mourners to and fro
> Kept treading—treading—till it seemed
> That Sense was breaking through—

Here, the HALF RHYME of the second and fourth lines aptly suggests the uneasiness evoked by the eerie situation.

Refrain

A **refrain** is a word, a phrase, a line, or a group of lines repeated at intervals in a poem. It is a common feature of folk ballads and of Elizabethan songs. For example, the clown Feste's song that concludes Shakespeare's *Twelfth Night* has the following refrain: "For the rain it raineth every day." Usually, as in that case, the refrain comes at the end of a STANZA. It may occur at other points in a poem, however, and it may contain variations on the original line.

A striking use of variation occurs in Langston Hughes's "Song for a Dark Girl," a bitter LYRIC about the lynching of a young black man. The refrain occurs not at the end but the beginning of the three QUATRAINS, and in the first and last STANZA it is identical:

> Way Down South in Dixie
> (Break the heart of me)

The middle STANZA, though, varies the second line of the refrain. It describes the sight that the NARRATOR finds so heartbreaking: the tortured corpse of her lover:

> Way Down South in Dixie
> (Bruised body high in air)

Sonnet ◀

The **sonnet** is a LYRIC poem, written in a single STANZA. It usually consists of fourteen lines of IAMBIC PENTAMETER. The RHYME SCHEME of the sonnet falls primarily into two types: the **Italian**, or **Petrarchan**, **sonnet** and the **English**, or **Shakespearean**, **sonnet**. The Petrarchan sonnet was named after Petrarch, the Italian poet who introduced the form in the early fourteenth century. It is divided into an opening **octave**—a group of eight lines—and a concluding **sestet**—a six-line unit. The RHYME SCHEME of the octave is usually fixed—*abba abba*, but that of the sestet may vary: *cde cde*, or *cdc cdc*, or *cdc dcd*.

The Petrarchan sonnet was introduced into English poetry by Sir Thomas Wyatt in the mid sixteenth century. His contemporary the Earl of Surrey changed the RHYME SCHEME to the format that has become known as the **English sonnet** or, after its most famous practitioner, the **Shakespearean sonnet**. It consists of three QUATRAINS and a final COUPLET, which rhyme *abab cdcd efef gg*.

The meaning in a sonnet follows the division of the parts. In the Petrarchan form, the octave usually describes a situation or a dilemma or poses a question. The sestet provides some sort of commentary or resolution. The **turn** (or **volta**, from the Italian for "turn") comes at the start of the sestet. Percy Bysshe Shelley's "Ozymandias," although highly irregular in its RHYME SCHEME, follows this typical division of the Petrarchan sonnet:

> I met a traveler from an antique land
> Who said: Two vast and trunkless legs of stone
> Stand in the desert. . . . Near them, on the sand,
> Half sunk, a shattered visage lies, whose frown,
> And wrinkled lip, and sneer of cold command,
> Tell that its sculptor well those passions read
> Which yet survive, stamped on these lifeless things,
> The hand that mocked them, and the heart that fed:
> And on the pedestal these words appear:
> "My name is Ozymandias, king of kings:
> Look on my works, ye Mighty, and despair!"
> Nothing beside remains. Round the decay
> Of that colossal wreck, boundless and bare
> The lone and level sands stretch far away.

The speaker opens the octave with a description of a monument like the sphinx, which the pharaoh Ramses II, called Ozymandias in Greek, had constructed of himself. The ancient face, half ruined, still expresses a "sneer of cold command." The second QUATRAIN reveals that the sculptor "mocked" (in the double sense of "imitated" and "ridiculed") such "passions" and the arrogant "heart" that "fed" them.

The VOLTA comes at the sestet, with the quotation of the inscription engraved on the statue's pedestal. It boasts of the monarch's "works" and asserts that even the "Mighty" can only "despair" at their grandeur. The sestet concludes, however, with an IRONIC description of the vast emptiness that now surrounds the "colossal wreck": the desert that has made a mockery of Ozymandias's vanity.

The structure of the Shakespearean sonnet conveys a different sort of reasoning than the Petrarchan. The three QUATRAINS usually present parallel images or variations on a theme. The TURN comes in the concluding COUPLET, which often either reverses the stance expressed earlier or provides a concise summary of it. A classic example is Shakespeare's Sonnet 30:

> When to the sessions[1] of sweet silent thought
> I summon up[2] remembrance of things past,
> I sigh the lack of many a thing I sought,
> And with old woes new wail my dear time's waste.
> Then can I drown an eye, unused to flow,
> For precious friends hid in death's dateless[3] night,
> And weep afresh love's long since cancelled woe,
> And moan the expense of many a vanished sight:
> Then can I grieve at grievances foregone,[4]
> And heavily from woe to woe tell[5] o'er
> The sad account[6] of fore-bemoanèd moan,
> Which I new pay as if not paid before.
>   But if the while I think on thee, dear friend,
>   All losses are restored and sorrows end.

In the first QUATRAIN the speaker begins by anticipating a pleasant, nostalgic recollection—"sweet silent thought"—of "things past." The ALLITERATED s sound is soothing. Instead, his conscience begins accusing him of missed opportunities and wasted efforts. He compares the process to court "sessions" in which he "summon[s] up" painful memories and newly laments these long past "woes."

The second QUATRAIN, which begins with the linking adverb "then," describes more specific sources of this anguish. It shifts the

---

1. Court hearings.
2. Call to court.
3. Endless.
4. Past.
5. Count up.
6. Financial tally.

metaphor to renewed accounts of past losses and debts. "Precious friends," now dead, the "woe" of an old, failed "love," and the "vanished sight" of other once valued things cause him to "moan" and "weep afresh."

The third QUATRAIN, which opens with another "then," continues this "sad account" of past "grievances." The repeated words (for example, "grieve" and "grievances," "woe" and "woe," "pay" and "paid") reinforce the melancholy tone. The largely END-STOPPED lines and the insistent stresses of the ENJAMBED line—"and heavily from woe to woe tell o'er / The sad account"—suggest the process of counting up past losses. The speaker is sadly listing once more his "fore-bemoanèd moans." The final COUPLET, however, marks an abrupt shift in attitude, signaled by the word "but." The speaker's sudden recollection of a "dear friend," addressed by the tender pronoun "thee," totally relieves his despair. It is not clear whether the beloved is deceased or just absent ("think on" is an ambiguous verb). In either case, the speaker is moved to the HYPERBOLIC statement that the "dear friend" serves as compensation for "all losses" and release from "all sorrows."

The sonnet has proven a popular and enduring poetic form. It both allows for variety in its subject matter and provides a structure that can inspire the imagination. For Petrarch, who addressed his sonnets to an idealized lady, Laura, the focus was romantic love. A number of sonneteers have followed his example, both in his choice of subject matter and in writing a **sonnet sequence**, a series of poems on the same topic. Examples include Shakespeare's own sonnets and, in the nineteenth century, Elizabeth Barrett Browning's *Sonnets from the Portuguese*. Countless other poets have used the sonnet for single poems and for strikingly diverse subjects: a religious struggle, as in John Donne's *Holy Sonnets*; a social or political crisis, as in William Wordsworth's "The World Is Too Much with Us" and Paul Laurence Dunbar's "Douglass"; a personal agony, as in Keats's "When I Have Fears That I May Cease to Be"; or a mythological concept, as in William Butler Yeats's "Leda and the Swan" and Edna St. Vincent Millay's "I Dreamed I Moved Among the Elysian Fields."

BLANK VERSE

Blank verse is unrhymed IAMBIC PENTAMETER. That is, it contains five FEET per line, each FOOT consisting of an UNSTRESSED followed by a STRESSED syllable. The verse is called "blank" because although it is in METER, it does not RHYME.

Blank verse is close to the rhythms of ordinary COLLOQUIAL English speech. It can also rise to a FORMAL, ceremonial style, however. The form allows for a variety of RHYTHMIC effects. The PAUSES, or lack of them, in mid-line and at the ends of lines take on special significance in blank verse poems.

Robert Frost uses a COLLOQUIAL blank verse in his narrative "Mending Wall." In mid-poem, the NARRATOR and a cranky neighbor meet to repair the stone wall between their properties, which has been damaged by winter weather:

> We keep the wall between us as we go.
> To each the boulders that have fallen to each.
> And some are loaves and some so nearly balls
> We have to use a spell to make them balance:
> "Stay where you are until our backs are turned!"   5
> We wear our fingers rough with handling them.
> Oh, just another kind of outdoor game,
> One on a side. It comes to little more:
> There where it is we do not need the wall:
> He is all pine and I am apple orchard.   10
> My apple trees will never get across
> And eat the cones under his pines, I tell him.
> He only says, "Good fences make good neighbors."

The blank verse is so understated that a reader might at first mistake the lines for prose. A closer look, however, shows Frost's masterful use of the form. The END-STOPPED lines, most of which contain an INDEPENDENT CLAUSE, reflect the neighbor's insistence on maintaining boundaries. The two sets of ENJAMBED lines describe the rebellious boulders (3–4) and dismiss the imaginary threat that the apple trees might graze the other farmer's pine cones (11–12). Those mocking lines suggest the narrator's wry conviction that walls between neighbors are futile and counterproductive.

In contrast, John Milton's use of blank verse in his epic *Paradise Lost* (1667) shows the FORMAL, eloquent capabilities of this poetic form. Here, for example, is the beginning of the "Invocation" to the Muse:

> Of man's first disobedience, and the fruit
> Of that forbidden tree[1] whose mortal taste
> Brought death into the world, and all our woe,
> With loss of Eden, till one greater Man[2]
> Restore us, and regain the blissful seat,   5

1. By God's commandment to Adam and Eve (Genesis 2.17).
2. Jesus Christ.

Sing, Heavenly Muse, that, on the secret top
Of Oreb, or of Sinai, didst inspire
That shepherd[3] who first taught the chosen seed
In the beginning how the Heavens and Earth
Rose out of Chaos: or, if Sion hill   10
Delight thee more, or Siloa's brook that flowed
Fast by the oracle of God, I thence
Invoke thy aid to my adventurous song,
That with no middle flight intends to soar,
Above th'Aonian mount,[4] while it pursues   15
Things unattempted yet in prose or rhyme.

The narrator begins by announcing his grand THEME: the fall of man
from God's grace, the "first disobedience" that resulted in Adam and
Eve's expulsion from the Garden of Eden and, in Judeo-Christian doc-
trine, was the cause of all subsequent earthly suffering.

Milton used several means to elevate the style: extensive
ENJAMBMENT—the opening sentence runs to sixteen lines; an APOS-
TROPHE to a classical Greek muse (line 6); FORMAL, learned DICTION;
and abundant classical and biblical ALLUSIONS.

The narrator himself defends his choice of blank verse as the
medium for expressing "things unattempted yet in prose or rhyme"
(16). As though that claim were not sufficient, Milton added a
preface to the second edition of the EPIC. In it he termed his METER
"English heroic verse" and cited the precedents of "Homer in
Greek" and "Virgil in Latin" as inspiring examples of "liberty" from
the "bondage of rhyming."

In addition to *Paradise Lost*, blank verse is used in other long
poems, such as William Wordsworth's *The Prelude*, Alfred, Lord Tennyson's *Idylls of the King*, and Seamus Heaney's *Station Island*, as well
as in countless short lyric poems.

During the Elizabethan era, blank verse also became the predominant form in English DRAMA. Shakespeare and his contemporaries rejected the tradition of writing in stiff, rather artificial
COUPLETS that had been used by their immediate predecessors. They
developed a dramatic form that sounded much more realistic.

At the same time, blank verse gave the dialogue greater formality
and structure than could have been achieved with prose. It created
a more flexible line than RHYMED COUPLETS would allow, and it also
elevated the style by suggesting that this was art, not real life.

---

3. Moses.
4. Home of the pagan Muses.

▼

Shakespeare's plays are not written entirely in blank verse; rather, they also include some passages in rhyme as well as others in prose. The rhyme tends to come in particular contexts: chants, such as those of the fairy king Oberon in *A Midsummer Night's Dream* and the witches in *Macbeth*, and in contests of wit, such as that between Romeo and Benvolio on the relative perfection of Rosaline (*Romeo and Juliet*). Shakespeare also often closes a scene or an act with a RHYMED COUPLET. In *Macbeth*, for example, the PROTAGONIST and his wife have been plotting the murder of the rightful king of Scotland. Macbeth seals their evil pact with the following couplet on the need for them to appear to be loyal and innocent:

> Away, and mock the time with fairest show.
> False face must hide what the false heart doth know.
>
> (I.7.81–82)

In a theater with such a limited set, the COUPLET could serve as a sort of verbal curtain on the action.

Shakespeare also included speeches in prose. That style may indicate a difference in social class: servants and lower-class characters tend to speak in prose—for example, the servingmen at the start of *Romeo and Juliet* and the Porter in *Macbeth*. That is not an absolute distinction, however. The aristocratic Mercutio suggests his nonchalance about love by speaking prose, and some of Prince Hamlet's most famous speeches, such as his bitter meditation on man as the mere "quintessence of dust," are in prose.

Also, a shift from prose to verse, or vice versa, can signal a change of mood in the speaker. For example, in *Othello* the villain Iago goes from COLLOQUIAL toying with the gullible Roderigo to eloquent SOLILOQUIES that reveal his evil schemes. For the Elizabethan actor, often required to perform multiple roles in a single season, blank verse was a valuable aid to memorization. It created a kind of metronome that underlay the words.

Many in Shakespeare's audience were illiterate, and for them written materials were rare and precious commodities. Therefore, they were accustomed to taking in information aurally and would have been alert to speakers' shifts between prose and verse. To aid modern readers in seeing such contrasts, editors space prose passages as in novels. They extend the lines all the way to the right margins and capitalize words only at the beginnings of sentences, not of lines. In contrast, they indicate that a speech is in verse by capitalizing the word at the beginning of each line and by leaving a wide right margin, as with poetry.

Editors also indent blank verse lines that are shared between two or more speakers and number them as one line. That spacing shows that the dialogue reflects a close meeting of the characters' minds. The reason for the shared line may be that the speakers are highly compatible, as in this exchange between Romeo and Juliet about plans for their secret wedding:

JULIET Romeo!
ROMEO   My nyas[5]?
JULIET   What o'clock tomorrow
        Shall I send to thee?
ROMEO   By the hour of nine.

Here, "Romeo!" "My nyas?" and "What o'clock tomorrow" represent one blank verse line, and "Shall I send to thee?" and "By the hour of nine" another. These two shared lines, in which each lover responds without pause to the other's words, show how closely attuned Romeo and Juliet are to one another's thoughts and rhythms. It is almost as if their heartbeats are synchronized.

A shared line may also show that one character is dominating the thoughts of the other. In this dialogue from *The Taming of the Shrew*, Petruchio, a brash fortune hunter, is attempting to court Katherine, the daughter of a wealthy man. She has the reputation of being a "shrew"—a rebellious, scolding woman—and Petruchio has made a bet that he can "tame" her. He immediately nicknames her "Kate" and tries to tease her into accepting his proposal. When he urges her not to "look so sour," she replies that that is her usual reaction to seeing a "crab," Elizabethan slang for a crab apple or sour person:

PETRUCHIO Why, here's no crab, and therefore look not sour.
KATHERINE There is, there is.
PETRUCHIO Then show it me.
KATHERINE   Had I a glass,[6] I would.
PETRUCHIO What, you mean my face?
KATHERINE   Well aimed, of such a
        young one.
PETRUCHIO Now, by Saint George, I am too young for you.
KATHERINE Yet you are withered.
PETRUCHIO   'Tis with cares.
KATHERINE   I care not.

---

5. Nestling hawk.
6. Mirror.

▼

The blank verse provides several indications that Kate is controlling this exchange. In the three shared lines (3, 5, and 7), she has the last word. Petruchio offers a challenge, asks a question, or gives an explanation. In each case, she responds with a SARCASTIC insult. A further sign of how thoroughly Kate is dominating the conversation is her short line "There is, there is," (2), which lacks the last three feet that would be needed to complete the IAMBIC PENTAMETER. Instead of the triumph that Petruchio expects, he has gotten further rebellion. The pause created by the short line implies that he is too shocked to reply immediately. When he does, with a rather feeble demand, Kate again snatches the lead by completing the blank verse line.

Blank verse has remained the preferred form for the relatively rare verse drama written in modern times, for example, T. S. Eliot's *Murder in the Cathedral*.

FREE VERSE (OPEN FORM VERSE)

In **free verse**, also called **open form verse**, the RHYTHMS are not organized into the regularity of METER. Most free verse also lacks RHYME. The term should not be confused with BLANK VERSE, unrhymed IAMBIC PENTAMETER.

What distinguishes free verse from prose? One of its main features is the deliberate division of the lines. Those may consist of very long units or of single words, and they may be divided in mid-sentence or even mid-word. As with poems in METER, the arrangement of the lines on the page is crucial to the meaning of free verse poems. That arrangement may include STANZA breaks, CAESURAS, and END-STOPPING and ENJAMBMENT to emphasize certain sounds and words. METER and RHYME SCHEME do not control such choices, as they do in **closed form** poems, such as those discussed above. Therefore, the poet must devise different means for creating coherence and emphasis.

The initial models for free verse poems were the psalms and the Song of Solomon in the King James Version of the Bible. In translating the Song of Solomon into English, scholars attempted to imitate the cadences of the original Hebrew:

I am the rose of Sharon, and the lily of the valleys
As the lily among the thorns, so is my love among the daughters.
As the apple tree among the trees of the wood, so is my beloved
    among the sons.
I sat down under his shadow with great delight, and his fruit
    was sweet to my taste.

He brought me to the banqueting house, and his banner over
    me was love.
Stay me with flagons, comfort me with apples: for I am sick of
    love.

The long lines, full of balance and ANAPHORA, have inspired such free
verse works as Walt Whitman's "Song of Myself":

I believe in you my soul, the other I am must not abase itself
    to you,
And you must not be abased to the other.

Loafe with me on the grass, loose the stop from your throat,
Not words, not music or rhyme I want, not custom or lecture,
    not even the best,
Only the lull I like, the hum of your valvèd voice.

Whitman's outlook is decidedly more secular—he is addressing not
a lover who embodies the divine but his own soul. Still, the poem
echoes the biblical song's lyrical rhythms and sensuous delights.
Poets using this melodic free verse style, based on biblical cadences,
have included Allen Ginsberg and Carl Sandburg.

An alternate style of free verse is the short, COLLOQUIAL, often
IRONIC form favored by such poets as E. E. Cummings, William Car-
los Williams, Elizabeth Bishop, and Langston Hughes. Here is the
beginning of Bishop's "The Fish":

I caught a tremendous fish
and held him beside the boat
half out of water, with my hook
fast in a corner of his mouth.
He didn't fight.
He hadn't fought at all.
He hung a grunting weight,
battered and venerable
and homely. Here and there
his brown skin hung in strips
like ancient wallpaper, and its pattern of darker brown
was like wallpaper:
shapes like full-blown roses
stained and lost through age.

The image of the fish at this point is decidedly unheroic. That outlook is suggested by the matter-of-fact tone and the "homely" SIMILE
of dilapidated wallpaper. The leisurely line containing that descrip-

▼

tion is longer than the rest, and it repeats the noun "wallpaper." In contrast, the earlier ANAPHORA, referring to the fish's lack of "fight," is emphasized by its IAMBIC beat and short, END-STOPPED line: "He didn't fight. / He hadn't fought at all." The fish is merely "a grunting weight," ready to be hauled in.

As the poem continues, however, the narrator looks more closely at her captive and notices the remnants of previous struggles: "five big hooks" lodged in his mouth and several dangling lines that snapped when "he got away." This is the conclusion:

> Like medals with their ribbons
> frayed and wavering,
> a five-haired beard of wisdom
> trailing from his aching jaw.
> I stared and stared
> and victory filled up
> the little rented boat,
> where oil had spread a rainbow
> around the rusted engine
> to the bailer rusted orange,
> the sun-cracked thwarts,
> the oarlocks on their strings,
> the gunnels—until everything
> was rainbow, rainbow, rainbow!
> And I let the fish go.

Here the SIMILE and METAPHOR suggest the fish's heroism. The remnants of previous fights are pictured as combat "medals" and the snapped lines as signs of ancient "wisdom." The commonplace details of the old "rented boat," listed in the long sentence that goes on for ten lines, get transformed by the narrator's awe at the fish's courage. In the triumphant final exclamation, the spilt oil becomes the "rainbow, rainbow, rainbow" of the fish's elevation. The last line, to which the entire account builds, derives its power from its simplicity and UNDERSTATEMENT.

Although the American poet Robert Frost famously dismissed writing in free verse as analogous to "playing tennis with the net down," free verse has become the most frequent poetic form in modern English poetry. It has been used with great effectiveness in works as diverse as Walt Whitman's "When Lilacs Last in the Dooryard Bloom'd" and T. S. Eliot's "The Waste Land." Indeed, numerous modern poets have mastered both CLOSED and OPEN FORMS—for example, D. H. Lawrence, T. S. Eliot, W. H. Auden, Sylvia Plath, and Adrienne Rich. As with any poem, reading free verse aloud or in the imagination, pausing where the poet has indicated a line break or a punctuation mark, attending to striking images and repeated sounds, may be the most direct means of responding to it.

EXERCISES: Poetic Forms

I. For each of the following passages:

- Name the STANZA pattern—COUPLET, QUATRAIN, BALLAD METER—or identify the REFRAIN.
- Explain why that term applies. *Note:* In some cases, more than one term may apply. If so, explain why both may be relevant.
- Describe how the STANZA pattern affects the TONE and the meaning of the passage.

1. I was angry with my friend:
    I told my wrath, my wrath did end.
    I was angry with my foe:
    I told it not, my wrath did grow.

    –WILLIAM BLAKE, "A Poison Tree"

2. Does the road wind up-hill all the way?
        Yes, to the very end.
    Will the day's journey take the whole long day?
        From morn to night, my friend.

    –CHRISTINA ROSSETTI, "Up-Hill"

3. This one was put in a jacket,
    This one was sent home,
    This one was given bread and meat
    But would eat none,
    And this one cried No No No No   5
    All day long.

    This one looked at the window
    As though it were a wall,
    This one saw things that were not there,
    This one things that were,   10
    And this one cried No No No No
    All day long.

    This one thought himself a bird,
    This one a dog,
    And this one thought himself a man,   15

> An ordinary man,
> And cried and cried No No No No
> All day long.
>
> —DONALD JUSTICE, "Counting the Mad"

4. Tell all the truth but tell it slant—
   Success in Circuit lies
   Too bright for our infirm Delight
   The Truth's superb surprise
   > —EMILY DICKINSON, "Tell all the truth but tell it slant—"

5. The old South Boston Aquarium stands
   in a Sahara of snow now. Its broken windows are boarded.
   The bronze weathervane cod has lost half its scales.
   The airy tanks are dry.
   > —ROBERT LOWELL, "For the Union Dead"

II. For two of the following poems or passages:

- Name the POETIC FORM exemplified—SONNET (PETRARCHAN or SHAKESPEAREAN), BLANK VERSE, or FREE VERSE.
- Identify the characteristics of the POETIC FORM.
- Explain how the POETIC FORM contributes to the TONE and meaning.

1. Pile the bodies high at Austerlitz[1] and Waterloo.
   Shovel them under and let me work—
   > I am the grass. I cover all.

   And pile them high at Gettysburg
   And pile them high at Ypres and Verdun.
   Shovel them under and let me work.
   Two years, ten years, and passengers ask the conductor:
   > What place is this?
   > Where are we now?

   > I am the grass.
   > Let me work.
   >
   > —CARL SANDBURG, "Grass"

---

1. The places mentioned were the sites of major battles in the Napoleonic Wars, the Civil War, and World War I.

2. Since there's no help, come let us kiss and part;
   Nay, I have done, you get no more of me,
   And I am glad, yea glad with all my heart
   That thus so cleanly I myself can free;
   Shake hands forever, cancel all our vows,   5
   And when we meet at any time again
   Be it not seen in either of our brows
   That we one jot of former love retain.
   Now at the last gasp of love's latest breath,
   When, his pulse failing, Passion speechless lies,   10
   When Faith is kneeling by his bed of death,
   And Innocence is closing up his eyes,
      Now if thou wouldst, when all have given him over,
      From death to life thou mightst him yet recover.

                              —MICHAEL DRAYTON, "Since there's no help,
                                              come let us kiss and part"

3. This living hand, now warm and capable
   Of earnest grasping, would, if it were cold
   And in the icy silence of the tomb,
   So haunt thy days and chill thy dreaming nights
   That thou wouldst wish thine own heart dry of blood   5
   So in my veins red life might stream again,
   And thou be conscience-calmed—see here it is—
   I hold it towards you.

                              —JOHN KEATS, "This Living Hand"

4.

   MACBETH I have done the deed. Didst thou not hear a noise?
   LADY MACBETH I heard the owl scream and the crickets cry.
      Did not you speak?
   MACBETH   When?
   LADY MACBETH   Now.
   MACBETH   As I descended?
   LADY MACBETH Ay.
   MACBETH   Hark!—Who lies i'th' second chamber?
   LADY MACBETH Donalbain.
   MACBETH   This is a sorry sight. [Looks at his hands.]
   LADY MACBETH A foolish thought, to say a sorry sight.

                              —WILLIAM SHAKESPEARE, Macbeth

Permissions Acknowledgments

Index of Terms

▼

▼